LETTERHEAD & LOGO DESIGN 8

ROCKPORT

First paperback published in the United States of America by
Rockport Publishers, Inc.
33 Commercial Street
Gloucester, Massachusetts 01930-5089
Telephone: (978) 282-9590
Fax: (978) 283-2742
www.rockpub.com

ISBN-13: 978-1-59253-131-8
ISBN-10: 1-59253-131-8

10 9 8 7 6 5 4

Design and Typography: Top Design Studio, Los Angeles, www.topdesign.com

Printed in China

LETTERHEAD & LOGO DESIGN

TOP DESIGN STUDIO, LOS ANGELES

8

GLOUCESTER MASSACHUSETTS

ROCKPORT PUBLISHERS

CONTENTS

"style

is a simple way of saying complicated things."

—JEAN COCTEAU

INTRODUCTION

A graphic designer's job is to successfully represent the client's message visually. At Top Design, we believe that effective design is grounded in simplicity; that economy of design prevents visual overload, revealing the distinct personality of the client and the message they wish to impart. Much of the work selected for this book relies on the power of subtlety to convey the style and sensibility of both client and designer.

The selection process was a collaborative effort — inspiring, exciting, and at times, daunting—as we culled approximately 500 pieces from more than 1,500 impressive entries submitted by designers worldwide. The work appearing in this book met our benchmarks of outstanding design through the use of spare, elegant typography and striking bold and neutral color palettes, as well as the expert handling of design elements throughout the letterhead systems. Each logo chosen to appear successfully communicates the intention and personality of the client it represents, through the use of icons, symbols, hand-rendered illustration, and typography.

We hope this book provides enjoyment to the casual reader and inspires fresh, creative solutions for designers worldwide.

top

Top Design Studio is a Los Angeles–based graphic design firm, established in 1991 by Peleg Top, principal and creative director. Following Peleg's passion for well-crafted logos and brand identities, Top Design Studio quickly gained status in the design community. Prestigious clients in the music and entertainment industries as well as not-for-profit organizations contributed to the studio's success and growing reputation. Peleg serves as chair of the Grammy Awards album packaging committee and is past president of the Graphic Artists Guild, southern California chapter. Top Design Studio has been featured in such major design publications as *Print*, *HOW*, and *Communication Arts*, and has received numerous awards for design excellence.

TOP DESIGN STUDIO » 11108 RIVERSIDE DRIVE, LOS ANGELES, CA, 91602 » WWW.TOPDESIGN.COM

1

2

3

4

5

1 **THE RECORDING ACADEMY** | GRAMMY AWARDS TELECAST LOGO

2 **RENDEZVOUS ENTERTAINMENT** | RECORD COMPANY LOGO

3 **GK COMMUNICATIONS** | PR AGENCY LOGO

4 **UNITARIAN UNIVERSALIST CHURCH** | LOGO FOR VERDUGO HILLS, CALIFORNIA CHURCH

5 **RESPONSE** | LOGO FOR JEWISH GAY FAMILY SUPPORT GROUP

inVision } coaching for the creative professional

1801 Dove St. Suite 104
Newport Beach, CA 92660
Tel 949.752.5758
Fax 949.833.3367
www.getinvision.com

u think you cannot do. —eleanor roosevelt

inVision.

inVision } 1801 Dove St. Suite 104
Newport Beach, CA 92660

inVision } coaching for the creative professional

RaShelle S. Westcott
Creative Coach
rashelle@getinvision.com

} 1801 Dove St. Suite 104
Newport Beach, CA 92660
Tel 949.752.5758
Fax 949.833.3367
www.getinvision.com

INVISION | LOGO AND LETTERHEAD SYSTEM FOR CREATIVE BUSINESS COACHING FIRM

MARCELO COELHO PHOTOGRAPHY
8800 Venice Boulevard Suite 202 Los Angeles, California 90034
telephone 310.204.4244 facsimile 310.204.4216
email info@marcelocoelho.com web www.marcelocoelho.com

MARCELO COELHO PHOTOGRAPHY
8800 Venice Boulevard Suite 202 Los Angeles, California 90034
telephone 310.204.4244 facsimile 310.204.4216
email info@marcelocoelho.com web www.marcelocoelho.com

an encyclopedia of gay, lesbian, bisexual, transgender & queer culture

an encyclopedia of gay, lesbian, bisexual, transgender & queer culture

an encyclopedia of gay, lesbian, bisexual, transgender & queer culture

an encyclopedia of gay, lesbian, bisexual, transgender & queer culture

1130 west adams street, chicago, illinois 60607
phone: 312 243 6562 fax: 312 243 8533

www.glbtq.com

www.glbtq.com

www.glbtq.com 1130 west adams street, chicago, illinois 60607 phone: 312 243 6562 fax: 312 243 8533

GLBTQ | LOGO AND IDENTITY FOR AN ONLINE GAY, LESBIAN, TRANSGENDER, & QUEER CULTURE WEBSITE

1 **BERLIN**

2 **ROCKTAILS**

3 **ZADE**

4 **LOS ANGELES CHAPTER**
RECORDING ACADEMY MEMBERSHIP AWARDS

1 **BERLIN** | LOGO FOR BAND IDENTITY
2 **ROCKTAILS** | LOGO FOR MUSIC INDUSTRY NETWORKING EVENT
3 **ZADE** | LOGO FOR RECORDING ARTIST IDENTITY
4 **THE RECORDING ACADEMY** | LOGO FOR ANNUAL MEMBERSHIP LUNCHEON AWARDS

PROFESSIONAL SERVICES

better than roses ...uitgever

Sabien Ebeling Koning
06 224 187 50

Nadja Wilderink
06 516 159 98

Rubensstraat 72¹
1077 NA Amsterdam

fax 020 87 22 478
e-mail mail@betterthanroses.nl
www.betterthanroses.nl

better than roses ...uitgever

Sabien Ebeling Koning 06 224 187 50
Nadja Wilderink 06 516 159 98

Rubensstraat 72¹
1077 NA Amsterdam

fax 020 87 22 478
e-mail mail@betterthanroses.nl
www.betterthanroses.nl

ING Bank 68 055 2154
KvK 34122831

HYBRID

70 Federal Street
Boston Massachusetts
02110

Telephone
617 728 · 4442

Telefax
617 728 · 4448

NASSAR DESIGN | ART DIRECTOR **NÉLIDA NASSAR** | DESIGNER **MARGARITA ENCOMIENDA** | CLIENT **HYBRID**

TYLER CARTIER   1200 POST ALLEY / SEATTLE, WA 98101   T 206.467.1174   F 206.343.0705   E TYLER@STRIKEPLATE.COM

WWW.STRIKEPLATE.COM

WORDS WITH CREATIVE SPARK

WWW.STRIKEPLATE.COM

PLATFORM CREATIVE | ART DIRECTOR **ROBERT DIETZ** | DESIGNER **RENEE YANCY** | CLIENT **STRIKEPLATE, TYLER CARTIER**

1508

DIGITAL KOMMUNIKATION

1508.DK A/S
Klosterstræde 23,4.
1157 København K
Danmark

T 7025 1508
F 7027 1508
info@1508.dk
www.1508.dk

A2-GRAPHICS/SW/HK | ART DIRECTORS SCOTT WILLIAMS, HENRIK KUBEL | CLIENT 1508

1 Expand Beyond™

2

3

4 HATCH

1 **LISKA + ASSOCIATES** | ART DIRECTOR **STEVE LISKA** | DESIGNERS **RUDI BACKART, STEVE LISKA** | CLIENT **EXPAND BEYOND**
2 **I. PARIS DESIGN** | ART DIRECTOR **ISAAC PARIS** | CLIENT **CITY PLUMBING, INC.**
3 **SAYLES GRAPHIC DESIGN** | ART DIRECTOR **JOHN SAYLES** | CLIENT **CATCH SOME RAYZ**
4 **GOTTSCHALK + ASH INTERNATIONAL** | ART DIRECTOR **STUART ASH** | DESIGNER **SONIA CHOW** | CLIENT **HATCH DESIGN INC.**

John Wehmann
john@thinkdesign.net

thinkdesign
and communications

407 N. Washington Street   Suite 102   Falls Church, VA 22046
tel: 703.237.0045   **fax:** 703.237.7538   **web:** www.thinkdesign.net

thinkdesign
and communications
407 North Washington Street, Suite 102
Falls Church, VA 22046

407 North Washington Street   Suite 102   Falls Church, Virginia 22046   tel: 703.237.0045   fax: 703.237.7538   web: www.thinkdesign.net

THINKDESIGN & COMMUNICATIONS | ART DIRECTOR **JIM GARZIONE** | DESIGNERS **JOHN WEHMANN, KRISTEN ULLRICH** | CLIENT **THINKDESIGN**

MONDERER DESIGN

2067 Massachusetts Avenue
Cambridge, MA 02140-1337

617 661 6125 FAX 661 6126
www.monderer.com

> Design + Visual Communications

RED DESIGN | ART DIRECTORS **ED TEMPLETON, HAMISH MAKGIU** | DESIGNER **RED DESIGN** | CLIENT **RED DESIGN**

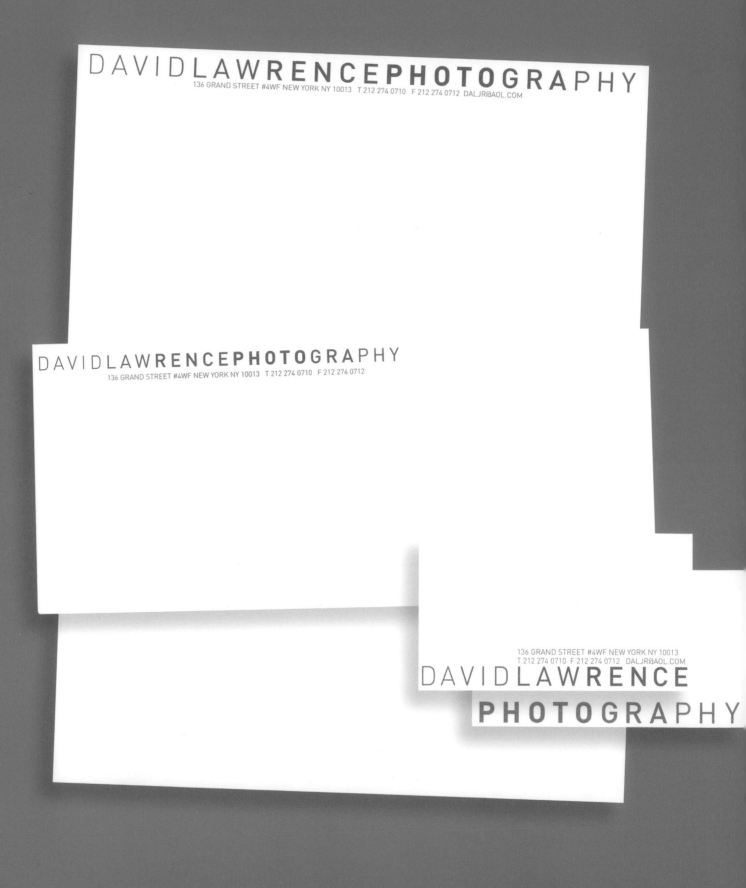

Our de Young

M.H. de Young Memorial Museum
Administrative Offices, 233 Post Street
San Francisco, California 94108

BALANCE DESIGN | ART DIRECTOR CAREY JONES | CLIENT BALANCE DESIGN

115 N 1st Street 2nd Floor
Minneapolis, MN 55401
www.rubincordaro.com

612 343 0011 phone
612 343 0012 fax

o
Rubin
Cordaro
Design

o
Rubin
Cordaro
Design

115 N 1st Street 2nd Floor
Minneapolis, MN 55401

Bruce Rubin

612 343 0011 phone
612 343 0012 fax
b.rubin@rubincordaro.com

o
Rubin
Cordaro
Design

115 N 1st Street 2nd Floor
Minneapolis, MN 55401
www.rubincordaro.com

115 N 1st Street 2nd Floor
Minneapolis, MN 55401
www.rubincordaro.com

o
Rubin
Cordaro
Design

115 N 1st Street 2nd Floor
Minneapolis, MN 55401
www.rubincordaro.com

o
Rubin
Cordaro
Design

115 N 1st Street 2nd Floor
Minneapolis, MN 55401
www.rubincordaro.com

o
Rubin
Cordaro
Design

RUBIN CORDARO DESIGN | ART DIRECTOR BRUCE RUBIN | DESIGNER JIM CORDARO | CLIENT RUBIN CORDARO DESIGN

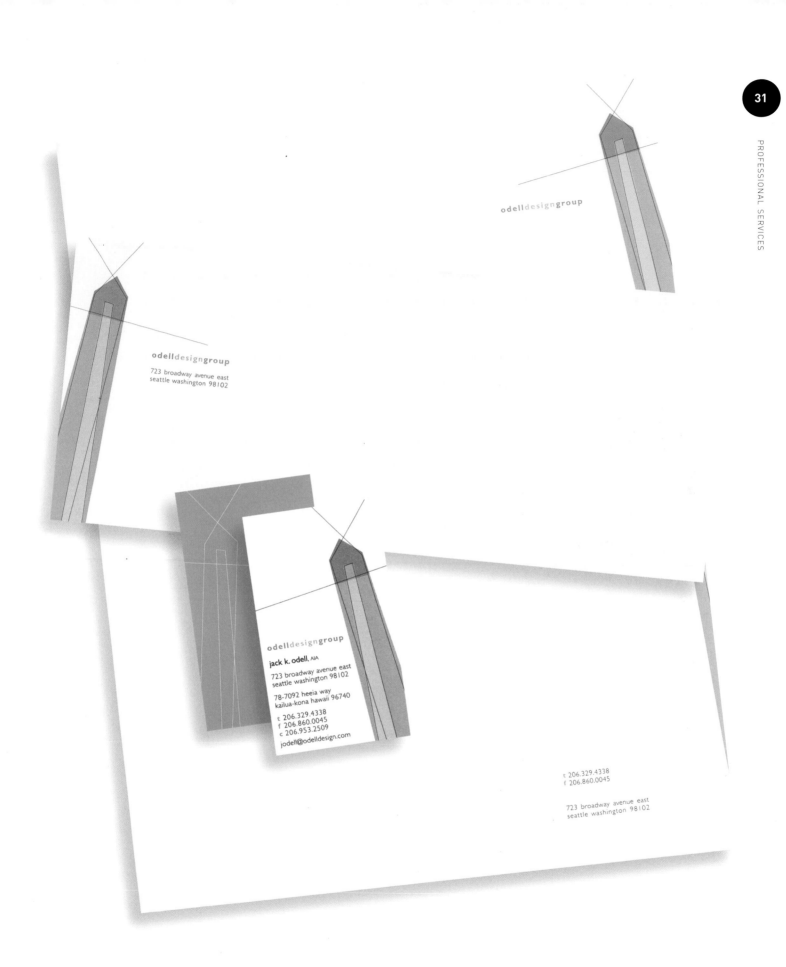

odelldesigngroup

odelldesigngroup
723 broadway avenue east
seattle washington 98102

odelldesigngroup

jack k. odell, AIA

723 broadway avenue east
seattle washington 98102

78-7092 heeia way
kailua-kona hawaii 96740

t 206.329.4338
f 206.860.0045
c 206.953.2509
jodell@odelldesign.com

t 206.329.4338
f 206.860.0045

723 broadway avenue east
seattle washington 98102

MONSTER DESIGN | ART DIRECTORS **HANNAH WYGAL, THERESA VERANTH** | DESIGNER **HANNAH WYGAL** | CLIENT **ODELL DESIGN GROUP**

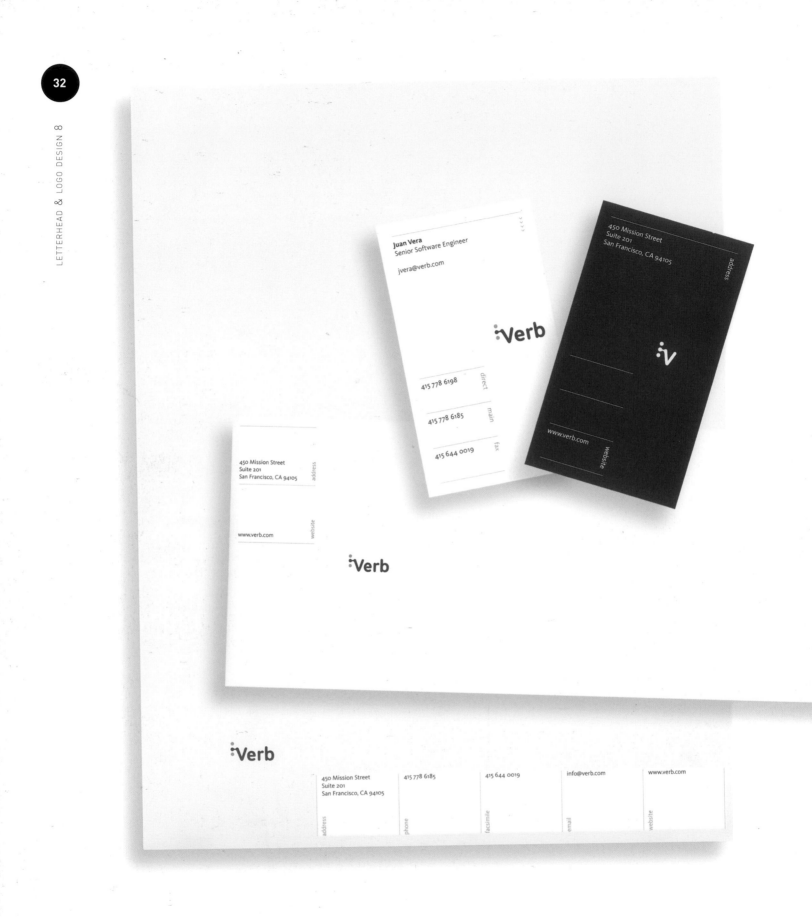

METHOD | ART DIRECTORS **MICHAEL ABBINK, PATRICK NEWBERY** | DESIGNERS **OLIVER CHETELAT, BETHANY KOBY, MIKE ABBINK** | CLIENT **VERB**

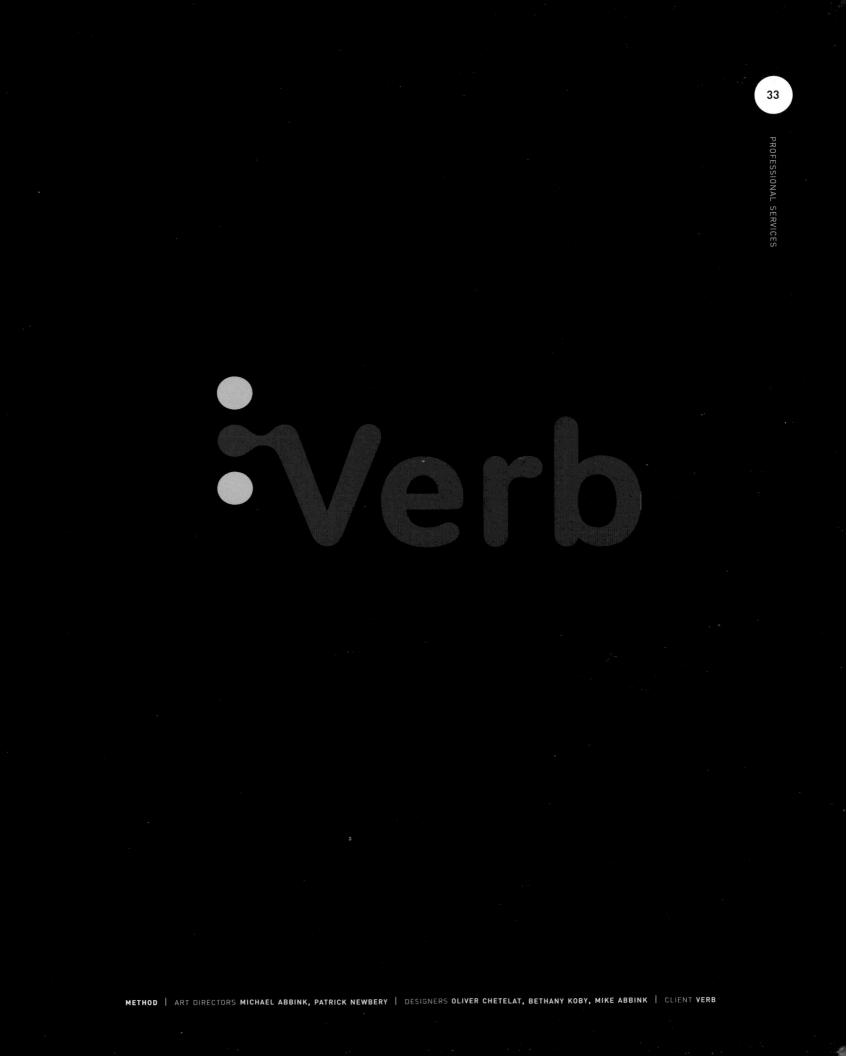

BURD & PATTERSON
GRAPHIC DESIGN STUDIO

BURD & PATTERSON
GRAPHIC DESIGN STUDIO

BURD & PATTERSON
GRAPHIC DESIGN STUDIO

2223 Grand Avenue Unit 4
West Des Moines, Iowa 50265
cell 515 710 9400
home studio 515 256 9400
brian@burdandpatterson.com
www.burdandpatterson.com

BRIAN C. PATTERSON
Client Relations Director

2223 Grand Avenue Unit 4 · West Des Moines, Iowa 50265 · 515-710-9400
info@burdandpatterson.com · www.burdandpatterson.com

BURD & PATTERSON | ART DIRECTORS **TRENTON BURD, BRIAN PATTERSON** | DESIGNER **TRENTON BURD** | CLIENT **BURD & PATTERSON**

ax/iz financial solutions
strategic - unique - proven

ax/iz financial solutions
strategic - unique - proven

Martin Maretzki, RHU
axiz@sympatico.ca

t 905 521 2817   f 905 521 2838

100 King St. W., Suite 1400
Hamilton, ON L8P 1A2

ax/iz financial solutions
strategic - unique - proven

Living Benefits

t 905 521 2817   f 905 521 2838

100 King St. W., Suite 1400
Hamilton, ON L8P 1A2

THE RIORDON DESIGN GROUP | DESIGNER **AMY MONTGOMERY** | CLIENT **AX/IZ FINANCIAL SOLUTIONS** | ART DIRECTOR **DAN WHEATON**

1

2

3

1 **FRESH BRAND, INC.** | ART DIRECTOR **MARCEL VENTER** | CLIENT **CAPITAL TITLE**
2 **FUSZION COLLABORATIVE** | ART DIRECTOR **TONY FLETCHER** | DESIGNERS **TONY FLETCHER, EMILY CARR** | CLIENT **PROPEL VENTURES**
3 **PAPER HAT DESIGN WORKS** | DESIGNER **TOM LYONS** | CLIENT **FOUR PRODUCTION SOLUTIONS**

AFTERHOURS GROUP | ART DIRECTOR LANS BRAHMANTYO | DESIGNER FEDRA CARINA | CLIENT AFTERHOURS GROUP

Telephone
020 8783 1177
Facsimile
020 8783 1188

www.blaze.uk.com

Blaze Professional
Systems Ltd
Millennium House
7 High Street
Hampton
Middlesex
TW12 2SA
United Kingdom

blaze

Blaze Professional Systems Ltd Registered in England Number: 3126871. Company VAT Number: GB 671 8257 14

WILSON HARVEY | ART DIRECTOR DANIEL ELLIOTT | CLIENT BLAZE SYSTEMS

DANIEL ELLIOTT | ART DIRECTOR **DANIEL ELLIOTT** | CLIENT **BLAZE SYSTEMS**

LIFE'S {ESSENTIALS}

2 DILLON ST
BLENHEIM
NEW ZEALAND

T/F: 03 578 7472
E: lifes.essentials@paradise.net.nz

LIFE'S {ESSENTIALS}

2 DILLON ST
BLENHEIM
NEW ZEALAND

T/F: 03 578 7472
E: lifes.essentials@paradise.net.nz

> CONSULT > COOK > COMPUTE > CREATE >

1

FRESHBRAND

3

PARADIGM
PUBLISHING GROUP

4

the
ESPRESSO
GOURMET

1 **FRESHBRAND, INC.** | ART DIRECTOR **MARCEL VENTER** | CLIENT **FRESHBRAND**

2 **YES DESIGN** | ART DIRECTOR **YVONNE SAKOWSKI** | CLIENT **REZAW-PLAST**

3 **GASKET** | ART DIRECTOR **MIKE CHRISTOFFEL** | DESIGNERS **MIKE CHRISTOFFEL, TODD HANSSON** | CLIENT **FIONA TUCKER**

4 **MORRIS CREATIVE INC.** | ART DIRECTOR **STEVEN MORRIS** | CLIENT **ESPRESSO GOURMET**

1

2

3

4

1 **LOVE COMMUNICATIONS** | ART DIRECTOR **PRESTON WOOD** | DESIGNERS **CRAIG LEE, PRESTON WOOD** | CLIENT **CRAIG LEE**
2 **UP DESIGN BUREAU** | ART DIRECTOR **TRAVIS BROWN** | CLIENT **CHRISTY PETERS**
3 **IRIDIUM, A DESIGN AGENCY** | ART DIRECTOR **MARIO L'ECUYER** | CLIENT **NEXWAVE CORPORATION**
4 **CATO PURNELL PARTNERS** | ART DIRECTOR **CATO PURNELL PARTNERS** | CLIENT **INFRATILE**

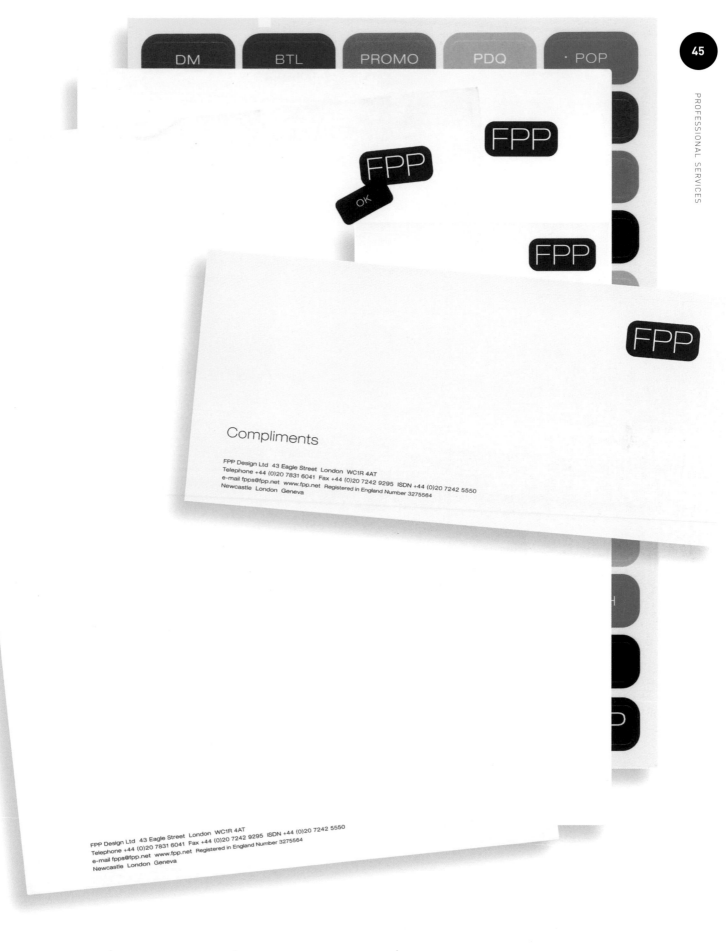

DEW GIBBONS | ART DIRECTOR **SHAUN DEW** | DESIGNER **SINE BRØGGER SØRENSEN** | CLIENT **FPP DESIGN**

Lela Tillem

127 EAST NINTH STREET NO. 705
LOS ANGELES CALIFORNIA 90015

T (213) 489 2391 F (213) 489 2394
LELA@SEASHOWROOM.COM

Sea
127 EAST NINTH STREET NO. 705 LOS ANGELES CALIFORNIA 90015

Sea

Sea
127 EAST NINTH STREET NO. 705 LOS ANGELES CALIFORNIA 90015 T (213) 489 2391 F (213) 489 2394

NICOLE CHIALA DESIGN | ART DIRECTOR NICOLE CHIALA | CLIENT SEA, LELA TILLEM

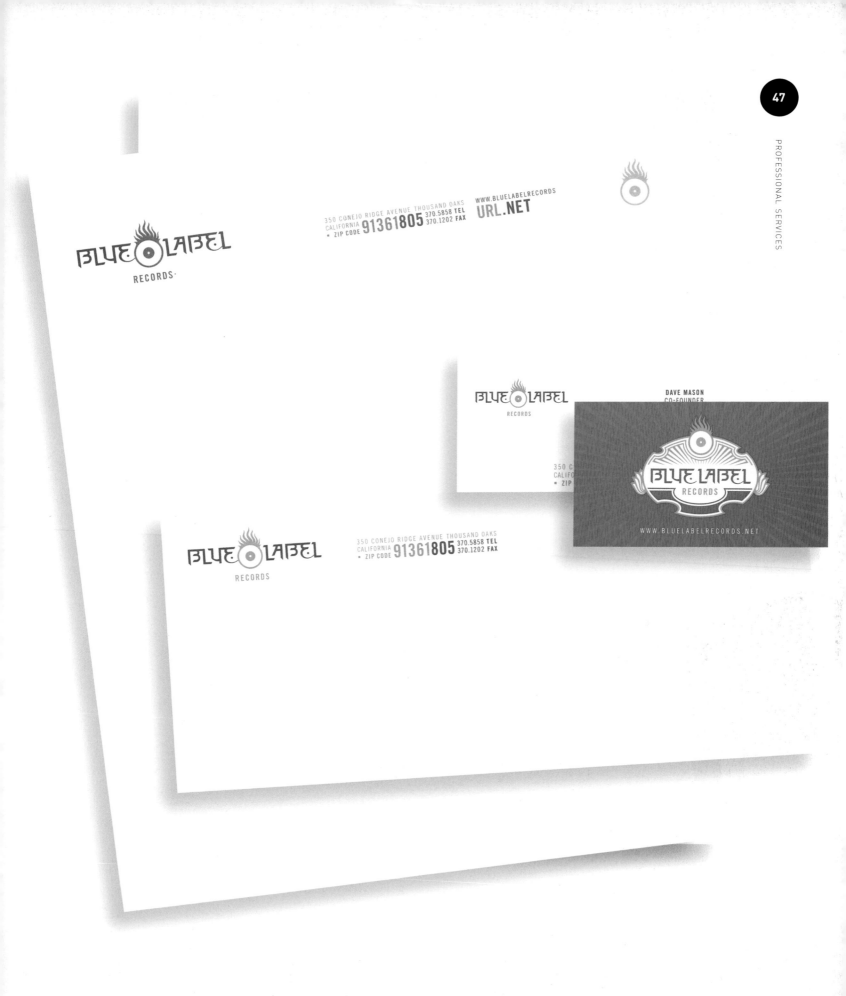

350 CONEJO RIDGE AVENUE THOUSAND OAKS
CALIFORNIA 370.5858 TEL
ZIP CODE 91361805 370.1202 FAX

WWW.BLUELABELRECORDS
URL.NET

DAVE MASON
CO-FOUNDER

WWW.BLUELABELRECORDS.NET

RKS DESIGN | ART DIRECTOR RAVI K. SAWHNEY | DESIGNER ALEX MARQUES | CLIENT BLUE LABEL RECORDS

1

safetyNETusa

2

replecs
FUTURE OF MESSAGING

3

FUSZION | COLLABORATIVE

1 FRESHBRAND, INC. | ART DIRECTOR MARCEL VENTER | CLIENT SAFETYNET USA.COM

2 STILRADAR | ART DIRECTOR RAPHAEL POHLAND, SIMONE WINTER | CLIENT REPLECS AG

3 FUSZION COLLABORATIVE | ART DIRECTORS RICHARD LEE HEFFNER, TONY FLETCHER | DESIGNER TONY FLETCHER | CLIENT FUSZION COLLABORATIVE

1

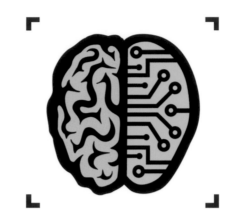

THINKSPACE

VENTURES BASED ON INTELLIGENT TECHNOLOGY

2

just ask!

3

1 **HONEY DESIGN** | ART DIRECTOR **ROBIN HONEY** | DESIGNER **JASON RECKER** | CLIENT **THINK SPACE**

2 **PACEY + PACEY** | ART DIRECTOR **ROBERT PACEY** | DESIGNER **MICHAEL PACEY** | CLIENT **JUST ASK!**

3 **RED STUDIOS** | ART DIRECTOR **RUBEN ESPARZA** | CLIENT **DEAN LARKEN DESIGN ARCHITECTS**

GWEN FRANCIS DESIGN GROUP | ART DIRECTOR GWEN FRANCIS | DESIGNER CHERYL RODER QUILL | CLIENT GROUNDSWELL

FINELINES

77 Walnut Street Unit 8   Peabody Massachusetts 01960   phone 978-977-7357   fax 978-977-7353   www.finelines.com

Pat King   Workroom Manager

FINELINES

phone 978-977-7357   ext 103
fax 978-977-7353   www.finelines.com

77 Walnut Street Unit 8   Peabody Massachusetts 01960

FINELINES

PLUS DESIGN INC. | ART DIRECTOR **ANITA MEYER** | DESIGNERS **ANITA MEYER, VIVIAN LAW** | CLIENT **FINELINES**

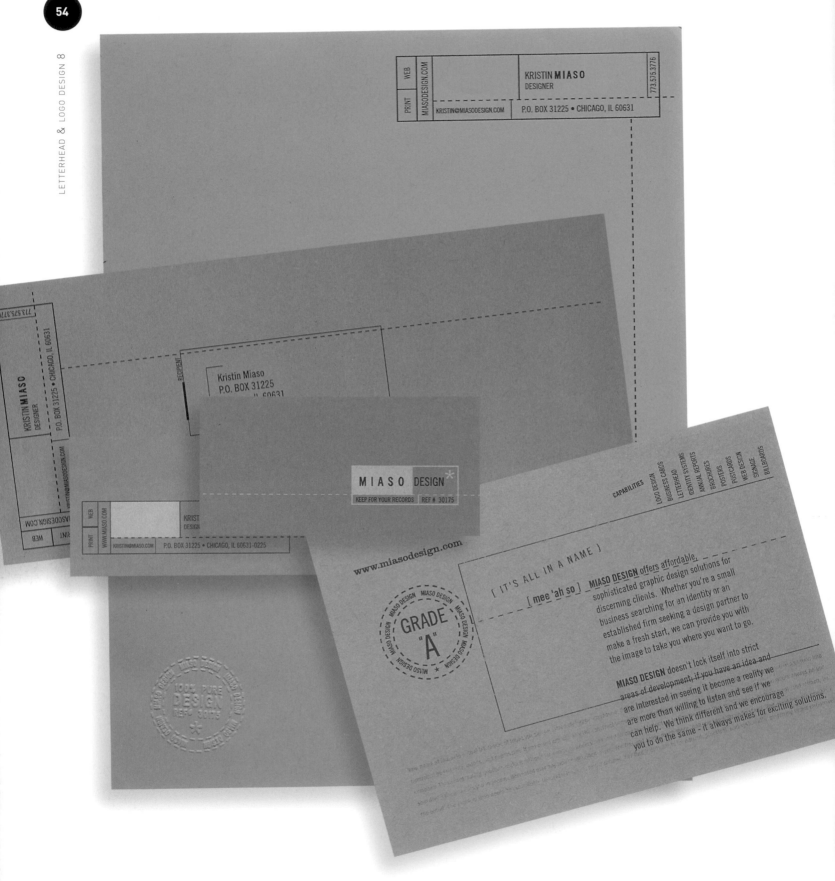

RE: SALZMAN DESIGNS | ART DIRECTOR IDA CHEINMAN | DESIGNERS IDA CHEINMAN, RICK SALZMAN | CLIENT APEX SEO

APEX

RE: SALZMAN DESIGNS | ART DIRECTOR IDA CHEINMAN | DESIGNERS IDA CHEINMAN, RICK SALZMAN | CLIENT APEX SEO

LEERS WEINZAPFEL ASSOCIATES

280 Summer Street
Boston, Massachusetts 02210
T 617.423.5711 **F** 617.482.7257

ARCHITECTS, INC.

Andrea P. Leers FAIA
Jane Weinzapfel FAIA
Josiah Stevenson AIA
Joe F. Pryse AIA

James E. Vogel AIA
Winifred Ann Stopps AIA
Margaret Minor AIA
Alex Adkins AIA
Joe M. Raia AIA
Alexander C. Carroll AIA

1

EFFORTLESSELEGANTEVENTS

So you can be the life of your party!

2

MAGPIE

COMMUNICATIONS

3

DOG'S
best friend

TONG DESIGN | ART DIRECTOR

1 **RED STUDIOS** | ART DIRECTOR **RUBEN ESPARZA** | CLIENT **KEVIN STALTER CO.**

2 **IRIDIUM, A DESIGN AGENCY** | ART DIRECTOR **JEAN-LUC DENAT** | CLIENT **MAGPIE COMMUNICAT**

3 **ML DESIGN** | CLIENT **DOG'S BEST FRIEND**

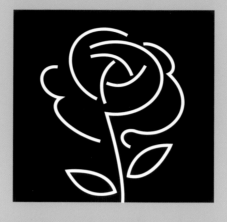

ROSTYLE

ROSTYLE

THE DIECKS GROUP | ART DIRECTORS MICHAEL WALDRON, BRIAN DIECKS | DESIGNER MICHAEL WALDRON | CLIENT SCANALOG

scanalog™

SCANALOG INC.

385 FARM TO M
BREWSTER,
TEL: 845
FAX: 84

WWW.

385 FARM TO MARKET RD. BREWSTER, NY 10509 | TEL: 845.279.7550 Fax: 845.278.4749
WWW.SCANALOG.COM

making IT personal

qual

making IT personal

■► networking
■► security
■► ~~~

qual
making IT personal

Patrick Stripp
Government Account Manager

Unit 10
Gatwick Metro Centre
Balcombe Road
Horley
Surrey
RH6 9GA

t: 01293 400 720
f: 01293 403 061

e: patrick@qual.co.uk
w: www.qual.co.uk

CPD | ART DIRECTOR **NIGEL BEECHY** | DESIGNERS **NIGEL BEECHY, FIONA CATT** | CLIENT **STUDENT DESIGN AWARDS**

iTAL!A
PARTNERS

iTAL!A
PARTNERS

italiap

MARV LeVee
Senior Vice President

308 WEST ERIE STREET
SUITE 400
CHICAGO, IL 60610

marvl@italiapartners.com

312.397.4324
312.397.4339

LOS ANGELES   DALLAS   CHICAGO

iTAL!A
PARTNERS

308 WEST ERIE STREET
SUITE 400
CHICAGO, IL 60610

LOS ANGELES   DALLAS   CHICAGO

308 WEST ERIE STREET SUITE 400 CHICAGO, IL 60610   312.397.9999   312.397.4339   italiapartners@com

LOS ANGELES   DALLAS   CHICAGO

VRONTIKIS DESIGN OFFICE | ART DIRECTOR PETRULA VRONTIKIS | DESIGNER REBECCA AU | CLIENT ITALIA PARTNERS

THOMAS BILLINGSLEY PHOTOGRAPHY

THOMAS BILLINGSLEY PHOTOGRAPHY

KARIZMA CULTURE | ART DIRECTOR **PERRY CHUA** | CLIENT **THOMAS BILLINGSLEY PHOTOGRAPHY**

LOCATED IN THE ANNEX / 45 ECCLES STREET OTTAWA ONTARIO K1R 6S3
613.567.7888 PHONE / 613.567.7528 FAX / csarchitect.com

Christopher Simmonds *ARCHITECT*

Christopher Simmonds *ARCHITECT*

WHITE SNOW ON VERMILLION BERRIES.
BUSY WINGS LOOSEN CRYSTAL SHOWER.

SILENCE.

LIGHT   AIR   WATER   EARTH

Christopher Simmonds *ARCHITECT*

THE ANNEX / 45 ECCLES STREET OTTAWA ONTARIO K1R 6S3
613.567.7888 X.22 PHONE / 613.567.7528 FAX / csarchitect.com
1.888.578.5678 TOLL FREE / pfiett@csarchitect.com

Pawel Fiett | B.Arch, OAA

IRIDIUM, A DESIGN AGENCY | ART DIRECTORS **JEAN-LUC DENAT, MARIO L'ECUYER** | DESIGNER **MARIO L'ECUYER** | CLIENT **CHRISTOPHER SIMMONDS**

1

2

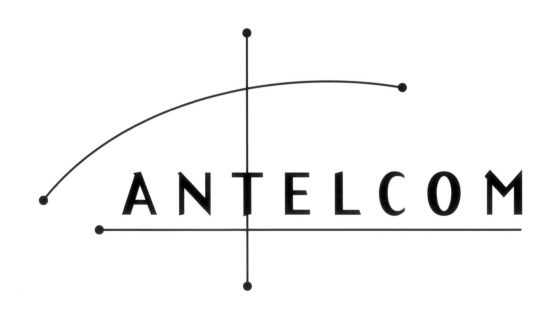

1 REACTOR ART + DESIGN | DESIGNERS PEBBLES CORREA, JERZY KOLACZ | CLIENT FUTURUS MANAGEMENT
2 MARC-ANTOINE HERRMANN | CLIENT ANTELCOM

Ant Hill
MARKETING

Public Relations   Advertising

Interactive

Direct Marketing

fig 1a - www.anthillmarketing.com

Ant Hill
MARKETING

P.O. Box 6585
Portland, Oregon 97228
ph (503) 236-3192
fx (503) 236-1186
kbrater@anthillmar

Ant Hill
MARKETING

P.O. Box 6585 · Portland, Oregon 97228 · ph (503) 236-3192 · fx (503) 236-1186

PURE DESIGN INC. | ART DIRECTOR JOHN FISHER | CLIENT ANT HILL MARKETING

THE DIECKS GROUP
530 BROADWAY, 9TH FLOOR
NEW YORK, NY 10012
STUDIO :: 212.226.7336
FAX :: 212.226.7937
www.diecksgroup.com

THE
DIECKS
GROUP
NEW YORK

THE
DIECKS
GROUP
NEW YORK

IECKS
DIRECTOR
GROUP
FLOOR
Y 10012
26.7336
FAX :: 212.226.7937

brian@diecksgroup.com / www.diecksgroup.com

THE DIECKS GROUP
530 BROADWAY, 9TH FLOOR
NEW YORK, NY 10012

THE
DIECKS
GROUP
NEW YORK

THE
CKS
ROUP
NEW YORK

LEMLEY DESIGN COMPANY
ADDRESS 8 BOSTON STREET, #11, SEATTLE, WA 98109, USA
TELEPHONE 206 285 6900 / FACSIMILE 206 285 6906 / INTERNET www.lemleydesign.com

THE **GRAPHIC LANGUAGE** OF POSITIONING

LEMLEY DESIGN COMPANY
KATIE DREKE Manager of Business Strategy
ADDRESS 8 BOSTON STREET, #11, SEATTLE, WA 98109, USA
TELEPHONE **206 285 6900** x207 / FACSIMILE 206 285 6906
INTERNET www.lemleydesign.com / EMAIL katie@lemleydesign.com

LEMELY DESIGN CO. | ART DIRECTOR **DAVID LEMLEY** | CLIENT **LEMLEY DESIGN**

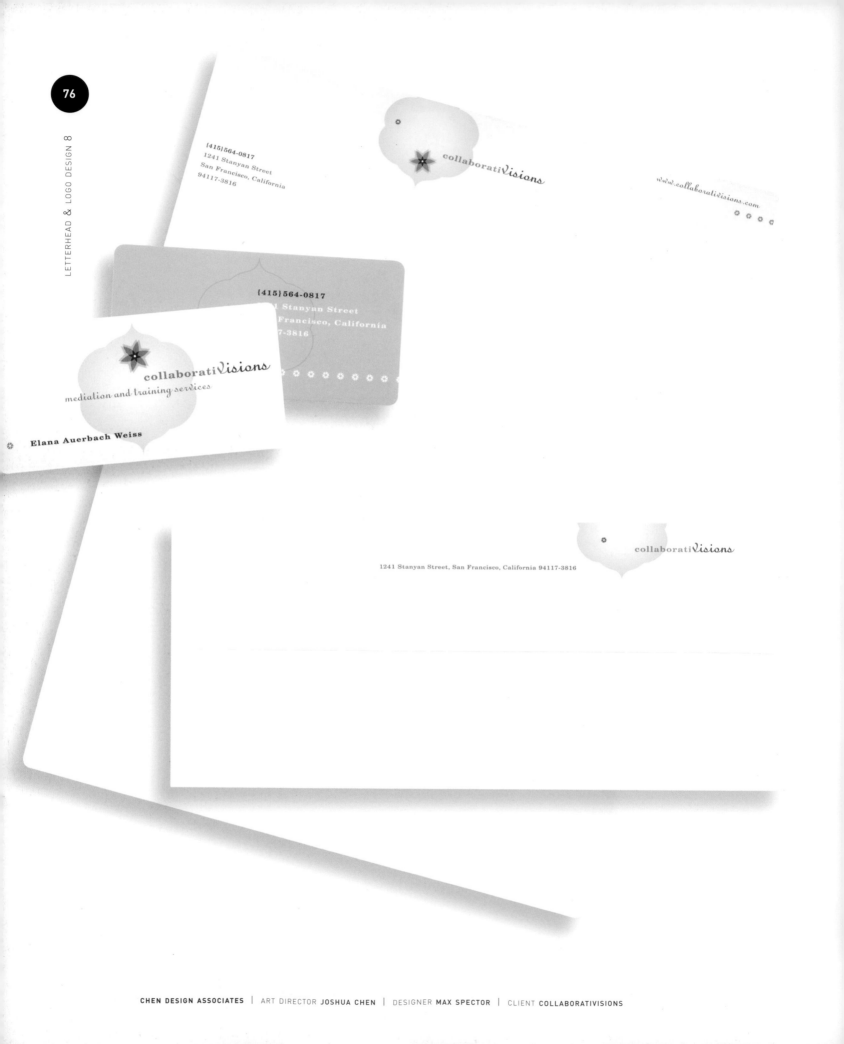

(415)564-0817
1241 Stanyan Street
San Francisco, California
94117-3816

collaboratiVisions

www.collaborativisions.com

(415)564-0817
Stanyan Street
Francisco, California
7-3816

collaboratiVisions
mediation and training services

Elana Auerbach Weiss

collaboratiVisions

1241 Stanyan Street, San Francisco, California 94117-3816

CHEN DESIGN ASSOCIATES | ART DIRECTOR JOSHUA CHEN | DESIGNER MAX SPECTOR | CLIENT COLLABORATIVISIONS

Wallace Church, Inc.
Strategic Brand Identity
330 East 48th Street
New York, NY 10017
212 755 2903

Wallace Church, Inc.
Strategic Brand Identity
330 East 48th Street
New York, NY 10017
T 212 755 2903
F 212 355 6872
www.wallacechurch.com

WALLACE CHURCH | ART DIRECTOR **STAN CHURCH** | DESIGNER **LAURENCE HAGGERTY** | CLIENT **WALLACE CHURCH INC.**

1

2

1 GOTT FOLK McCANN-ERIKSON | ART DIRECTOR EINAR GYLFASON | CLIENT SISSA PHOTOGRAPHY SCHOOL
2 LEWIS COMMUNICATIONS | ART DIRECTOR ROBERT FROEDGE | CLIENT STAGE POST VIDEO AND POST

Joos Luteijn
+31 627 424 878

Hamersveldseweg 56a   T +31 33 433 28 47   E joos@prepay.nl
3833 GS Leusden   F +31 33 433 34 45   S www.prepay.nl

CREATIVE SERVICES

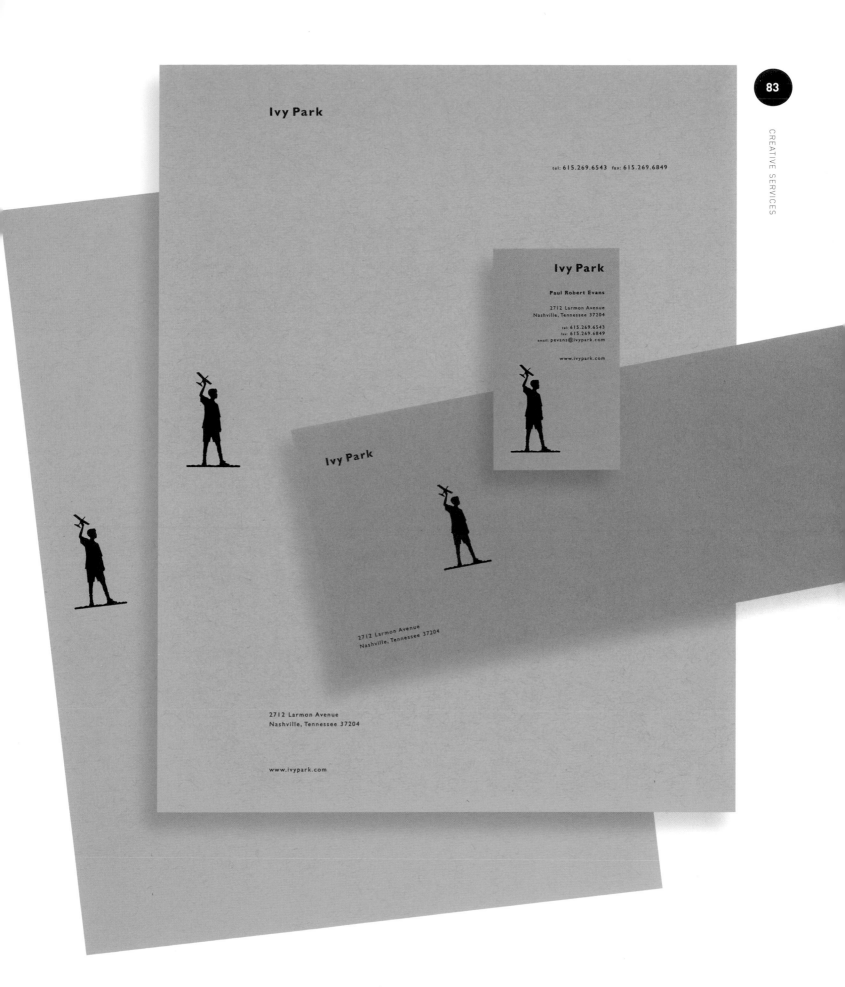

martinBattarchitects

Martin Batt

39 Wachusett Road

Needham

MA 02492

USA

Telephone 781 444 2747

Fax 781 444 0894

mbatt@martinbatt.com

martinBattarchitects

39 Wachusett Road

Needham

MA 02492

USA

Telephone 781 444 2747

Fax 781 444 0894

martin Batt architects LLC

martinBattarchitects

39 Wachusett Road

Needham

MA 02492

USA

Telephone 781 444 2747

Fax 781 444 0894

www.martinbatt.com

D. DESIGN | ART DIRECTOR **DEREK SAMUEL** | CLIENT **MARTIN BATT**

COLOUR: **anne** COLOUR: **parker** COLOUR: **decor**

Interior Decorating & Design
Tailored to Suit
Your Home, Your Tastes, Your Budget

JOB No. 016003

PO Box 363, Blenheim · T: 03 577 7567 · F: 03 578 9552 · M: 025 525 302 · E: anne.p@xtra.co.nz

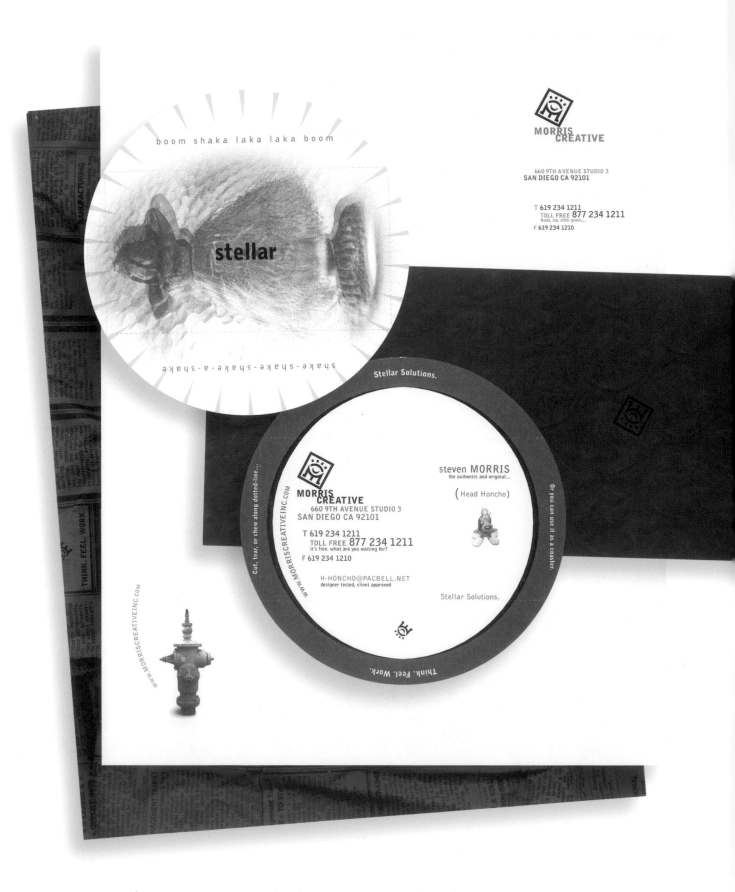

eMMA WILSON
DESIGN COMPANY

eMMA WILSON
DESIGN COMPANY

500 Aurora Avenue North
SEATTLE, WASHINGTON 98109

500 Aurora Avenue North
SEATTLE, WASHINGTON 98109
TEL 206/652-9928   FAX 206/965-2246   www.emmadesignco.com

EMMA WILSON DESIGN CO. | DESIGNER EMMA WILSON | CLIENT EMMA WILSON DESIGN CO.

HeadQuarter.net

HEAD QUARTER | ART DIRECTORS **MARTIN BOTT, PETER HEINZ** | CLIENT **HEAD QUARTER**

Jen Wink / PRINCIPAL
jwink@utilitydesign.net

Utility Design
434 Lafayette Street Suite B1
New York City 10003

Utility Design
434 Lafayette Street
Suite B1
New York City 10003
tel 212 674 4280
fax 212 420 9405

www.utilitydesign.net

Utility Design
434 Lafayette Street
Suite B1
New York City 10003
tel 212 674 4280
fax 212 420 9405

www.utilitydesign.net

Utility Design
434 Lafayette Street
Suite B1
New York City 10003
tel 212 674 4280
fax 212 420 9405

www.utilitydesign.net

blue

58 old compton street, london W1D 4UF
tel 020 7437 2626 fax 020 7439 2477
www.bluepp.co.uk

blue

blue

58 old compton street,
tel 020 7437 2626 fax 0

blue

blue

58 old compton street, london W1D 4UF
tel 020 7437 2626 fax 020 7439 2477
www.bluepp.co.uk

blue post production ltd. registered office: 100 fetter lane, london EC4A 1DD. no:2054062

WHY NOT ASSOCIATES | ART DIRECTOR WHY NOT ASSOCIATES | CLIENT BLUE POST PRODUCTION

HOLGER SCHEIBE

HOLGER SCHEIBE // PHOTOGRAPHY

HOLGER SCHEIBE

HAMBURG +49 40.430 41 75 // NEW YORK +1 212.213 95 39
HOLGERSCHEIBE@AOL.COM // WWW.HOLGERSCHEIBE.COM
GLASHÜTTENSTRASSE 38 // 20357 HAMBURG

HOLGER SCHEIBE // PHOTOGRAPHY

HAMBURG +49 40.430 41 75 // NEW YORK +1 212.213 95 39   GLASHÜTTENSTRASSE 38 // 20357 HAMBURG // FAX +49 40.432 26 14
HOLGERSCHEIBE@AOL.COM // WWW.HOLGERSCHEIBE.COM   DEUTSCHE BANK HAMBURG // KONTO 36 82 762 // BLZ 200 700 00

LE-PALMIER | ART DIRECTOR **ANDREAS PALM** | CLIENT **HOLGAR SCHEIBE PHOTOGRAPHY**

PAGE

DELIVER TO

IRIDIUM, A DESIGN AGENCY | ART DIRECTORS MARIO L'ECUYER, JEAN-LUC DENAT | DESIGNER MARIO L'ECUYER | CLIENT IRIDIUM, A DESIGN AGENCY

IRIDIUM

IRIDIUM, A DESIGN AGENCY | ART DIRECTORS MARIO L'ECUYER, JEAN-LUC DENAT | DESIGNER MARIO L'ECUYER | CLIENT IRIDIUM, A DESIGN AGENCY

Juan Carlos Fernández Espinosa
Director Creativo

i d e o g r a m a

t: (777) 313 8466 ext. 101
f: (777) 317 6436
jc@ideograma.com
Tabasco 414-11, Las Maravillas
Cuernavaca, México 62230
www.ideograma.com

IDEAS CON IDENTIDAD

las   Cuernavaca, México 62230   t: +52 (777) 313 8466   f: +52 (777) 317 6436   www.ideograma.com

en **ideas** claras y les damos forma a traves
de mensajes flexibles y relevantes. Ideamos
identidades corporativas y posicionamientos
exitosos apoyados en un esfuerzo integral,
en lo que denominamos **identidad global.**

i d e o g r a m a

i d e o g r a m a
IDEAS CON IDENTIDAD

Cuernavaca, México 62230   t: +52 (777) 313 8466   f: +52 (777) 317 6436   www.ideograma.com

En **Ideograma** creamos nombres,
posicionamientos e identidades
corporativas exitosas.

Convertimos sólidas estrategias
de negocio en **ideas** claras y les
damos forma mediante mensajes
flexibles y relevantes. Ideamos
marcas memorables y eficaces
apoyados en un esfuerzo integral,
en lo que denominamos
identidad global.

IDEAS CON IDENTIDAD

1

2

3 ALBUQUERQUE

4

1 **LISKA + ASSOCIATES** | ART DIRECTOR **STEVE LISKA** | DESIGNER **PAUL WONG** | CLIENT **SOTO DESIGNS**
2 **SAGMEISTER** | ART DIRECTOR **STEFAN SAGMEISTER** | DESIGNER **MATHIAS ERNSTBERGOR** | CLIENT **LOU REED**
3 **HAMBLY & WOOLLEY, INC.** | ART DIRECTOR **BOB HAMBLY** | DESIGNER **EMESE UNGAR** | CLIENT **LUIS ALBUQUERQUE**
4 **PUBLICIDAD GOMEZ CHICA** | ART DIRECTOR **SANTIAGO JARAMILLO** | CLIENT **TROPICO**

1

MULTIMEDIA

2

MICHAEL POWELL
Design & Art Direction

3

4

1 **CFX CREATIVE** | ART DIRECTOR **CARLY H. FRANKLIN** | CLIENT **CFX CREATIVE**

2 **MICHAEL POWELL DESIGN & ART DIRECTION** | ART DIRECTOR **MICHAEL POWELL** | CLIENT **MICHAEL POWELL DESIGN & ART DIRECTION**

3 **BEAULIEU CONCEPTS GRAPHIQUES INC.** | ART DIRECTOR **GILLES BEAULIEU** | CLIENT **LABORATOIRE DENTAIRE MONDOR**

4 **LLOYD'S GRAPHIC DESIGN AND COMMUNICATION** | ART DIRECTOR **ALEXANDER LLOYD** | CLIENT **GRANT FINCH**

N⁰. 27 HOXTON STREET
LONDON N1 6NH
TELEPHONE + 44 (0) 20 7613 3886
FAX + 44 (0) 20 7729 8500
EMAIL name@pennyrich.co.uk
www.pennyrich.co.uk

VAT NO. 627 9237 14

PENNYRICH

PENNYRICH

N⁰. 27 HOXTON STREET
LONDON N1 6NH
TELEPHONE + 44 (0) 20 7613 3886
FAX + 44 (0) 20 7729 8500
EMAIL penny@pennyrich.co.uk
www.pennyrich.co.uk

D. DESIGN | ART DIRECTOR **DEREK SAMUEL** | CLIENT **PENNY RICH**

PLATFORM CREATIVE GROUP | ART DIRECTOR **ROBERT DIETZ** | DESIGNERS **ROBERT DIETZ, TODD KARAM** | CLIENTS **KATHY THOMPSON, JIM KOON**

firebox *media*

firebox *media*
569 waller street
san francisco, ca
94117

569 waller street san francisco, ca 94117

firebox *media*

569 waller street   san francisco, ca   94117   t: 415.436.9997   www.fireboxmedia.com

Prisma Imaging
Colour reprographics

Unit Thirty Three
Westfield Trading Estate
Midsomer Norton
Radstock BA3 4BS

Telephone 01761 418867
Facsimile 01761 419464
Email prisma@dircon.co.uk
Registered No. 3202188

NORTH BANK | ART DIRECTOR **SIMON CRYER** | CLIENT **PRISMA REPROGRAPHICS**

unstable

MADE IN THE BUNDESREPUBLIK

TELEPHONE	TELEFAX	ISDN	ADDRESS
+49 (40) 432 948 - 0	+49 (40) 432 948 - 11	+49 (40) 432 948 - 31	Juliusstrasse 25	22769 Hamburg

FORK UNSTABLE MEDIA - 4RK (NY) (HH) (B)

E.MAIL: INFO@FORK.DE   HTTP://WWW.FORK.DE

MADE IN THE BUNDESREPUBLIK

(NY) (HH) (B)

FORK UNSTABLE MEDIA - 4RK

>> HAMBURG >> NEW

FORK UNSTABLE MEDIA

(NY) (HH) (B)

(NY)

MAIL	jeremy@fork.de	INTERNET	http://www.fork.de
ADDRESS	184 Kent Avenue Fifth floor. #5B Brooklyn, NY 11211	TELEPHONE	+1 (718) 384 1401
		TELEFAX	+1 (718) 384 1402

FORK NEW YORK

MADE IN THE BUNDESREPUBLIK

YELIZ ATILGAN PROJECT MANAGER O1

>> HAMBURG >> NEW YORK >> BERLIN

>> MOBILE CRYSTAL

NOW LOADING

BANK Deutsche Bank Hamburg | BLZ 200 700 24 KTO 322 10 66
Fork Unstable Media GmbH

MARIUS FAHRNER DESIGN | ART DIRECTOR **MARIUS FAHRNER** | CLIENT **FORK UNSTABLE MEDIA**

GARY BASEMAN | ART DIRECTOR **GARY BASEMAN** | DESIGNER **JILL VON HARTMANN** | CLIENT **GARY BASEMAN**

WHISTLER'S MUSIC

I.V. RECORDS

WHISTLER'S MUSIC PUBLISHING

WHISTLER'S MUSIC

I.V. RECORDS

WHISTLER'S MUSIC PUBLISHING

WHISTLER'S ENTERTAINMENT GROUP 1701 CHURCH STREET NASHVILLE TN 37203

WHISTLER'S ENTERTAINMENT GROUP 1701 CHURCH STREET NASHVILLE TN 37203 PHO: 615.320.1444 FAX: 615.320.0750

LEWIS **COMMUNICATIONS** | ART DIRECTOR **ROBERT FROEDGE** | CLIENT **WHISTLER'S ENTERTAINMENT GROUP**

kevduttonphotography

57 Dorchester Court
London
SE24 9QY

T/F 020 7274 3337
M 07973 113969
E kevdutton@aol.com

VAT reg 681 5010 56

WILSON HARVEY | ART DIRECTOR PAUL BURGESS | DESIGNER DAN ELLIOTT | CLIENT KEV DUTTON PHOTOGRAPHY

www.lepalmier.de

Le_Palmier

Andreas Palm Design

Le_Palmier
Andreas Palm Design
Große Brunnenstraße 63a

22763 Hamburg

www.lepalmier.de

Fon_040.460 690-61 : Fax_040.460 690-62
Große Brunnenstraße 63a : 22763 Hamburg
eMail_design@lepalmier.de

Andreas Palm Design

Le_Palmier

Fon_040.460 690-61 : Fax_040.460 690-62
Große Brunnenstraße 63a : D_22763 Hamburg
eMail_design@lepalmier.de

LE-PALMIER | ART DIRECTOR **ANDREAS PALM** | CLIENT **LE-PALMIER**

TESSER™
the smartest distance between two points℠

Debra Naeve
Graphic Designer
415.541.9999

the smartest
distance between two points℠

650 Delancey Street, Loft #404
San Francisco, CA 94107
t> 800.310.4400
f> 415.541.9699
e> debra.naeve@tesser.com

www.tesser.com

TESSER™
the smartest distance between two points℠

> I-BUILDING
> STRATEGIC BRANDING
> NEW VENTURES

(B)   **Tesser, Inc.** 650 Delancey Street, Loft #404   San Francisco, CA 94107   **t>** 800.310.4400   **f>** 415.541.9699   **w>** tesser.com

TESSER, INC. | ART DIRECTOR **TRE MUSCO** | DESIGNERS **KIMBERLY CROSS, SANDRINE ALBOUY** | CLIENT **TESSER, INC.**

ratio one.

WILSON HARVEY | ART DIRECTOR PAUL BURGESS | CLIENT RATIO ONE

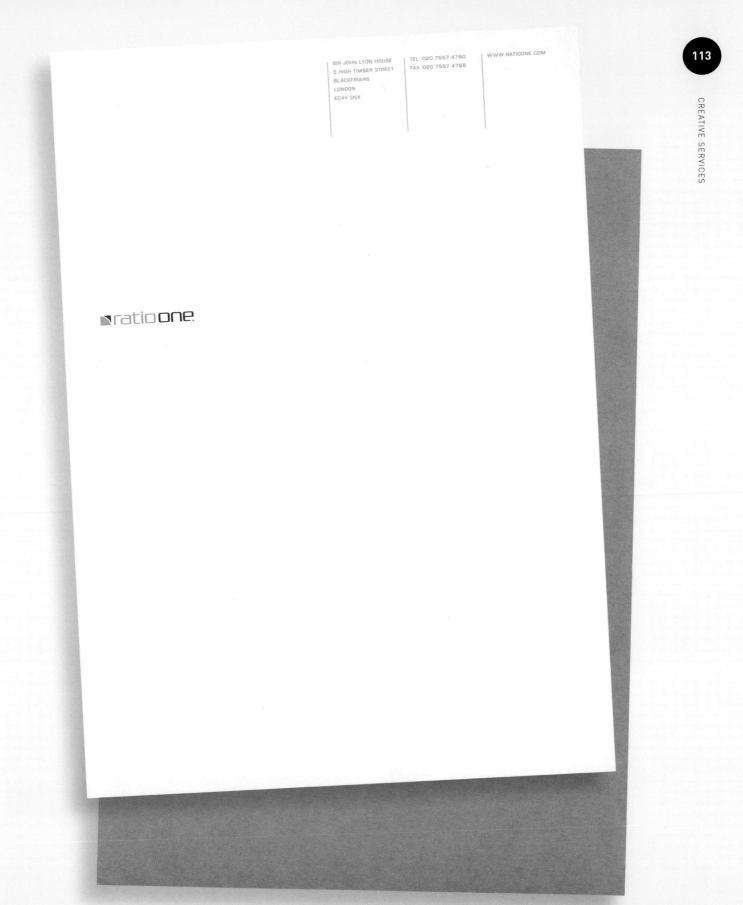

SIR JOHN LYON HOUSE
5 HIGH TIMBER STREET
BLACKFRIARS
LONDON
EC4V 3NX

TEL 020 7557 4760
FAX 020 7557 4768

WWW.RATIOONE.COM

WILSON HARVEY | ART DIRECTOR **PAUL BURGESS** | CLIENT **RATIO ONE**

tom & john ●
A DESIGN COLLABORATIVE ●

○ **ADDRESS :** 1298 HAIGHT STREET, no. 5
SAN FRANCISCO, CA 94117
TEL : 415 621 0444
FAX : 415 551 1220
EMAIL : TOMSIEU@PACBELL.NET
WEB : tom-john.com

○ **ADDRESS :** 1620 CASTRO STREET
SAN FRANCISCO, CA 94114
TEL : 415 641 5873
FAX : 415 824 1072
EMAIL : JOHN@IONIX.NET
WEB : tom-john.com

TOM & JOHN: ADC | ART DIRECTORS **TOM SIEU, JOHN GIVENS** | CLIENT **TOM & JOHN: ADC**

jmk Kommunikationsdesign / Goetheallee 19 (Laden) / 22765 Hamburg.

JMK KOMMUNIKATIONSDESIGN
URL www.zuckerschock.de / MAIL inbox@zuckerschock.de
OFFICE Goetheallee 19 (Laden) / 22765 Hamburg / Germany
PHONE 0049-40-38 08 38 61 / FAX-24 / ISDN sometimes / MOBILE always

JMK KOMMUNIKATIONSDESIGN
URL www.zuckerschock.de / MAIL inbox@zuckerschock.de
OFFICE Goetheallee 19 (Laden) / 22765 Hamburg / Germany
PHONE 0049-40-38 08 38 61 / FAX-24 / ISDN sometimes / MOBILE always

DUCKS DESIGN, HAMBURG | ART DIRECTOR **JAN M. KÜRZINGER** | CLIENT **JMK DESIGN, HAMBURG**

pink+purple public relations

pink+purple public relations

pink+purple public relations

Leinp
Tel.:+49(0)40-46

pink+purple

Leinpfad 80   22299 Hamburg
Telefon: 040-460 90 501   Telefax: 040-460 90 502
mail@pink-purple.de

Leinpfad 80   22299 Hamburg   Telefon:+49(0)40-460 90 501   Fax:+49(0)40-460 90 502   mail@pink-purple.de
Bankverbindung: Claudia Lüders   Deutsche Bank 24   Kto.: 2459 808-01   BLZ.: 200 700 24

MARIUS FAHRNER DESIGN | ART DIRECTOR **MARIUS FAHRNER** | CLIENT **CLAUDIA LÜDERS**

RETAIL, RESTAURANT, AND HOSPITALITY

1

2   3

1

2

1 PURE DESIGN INC. | ART DIRECTOR RACHELLE FISHER | DESIGNER JOHN FISHER | CLIENT IDYLWILDE FLIES
2 GILLESPIE DESIGN INC. | ART DIRECTOR MAUREEN GILLESPIE | DESIGNER LIZ SCHENKEL | CLIENT WENDY AND AMY (BABY STATIONERY)

ENERGY ENERGY DESIGN | ART DIRECTOR LESLIE GUIDICE | DESIGNERS STACY GUIDICE, JEANETTE ARAMBURU | CLIENT ACME CHOPHOUSE

address: 7373 beverly blvd. los angeles, ca 90036 **phone:** 323.931.4442 **fax:** 323.931.9992 **www:** onaspa.com

ona

candace farrell

address: 7373 beverly blvd. los angeles,
california 90036 phone: 323.931.4442
fax: 323.931.9992 www: onaspa.com

good

ona

ona

7373 beverly blvd. **los angeles,** ca **90036**

ona

1

2

3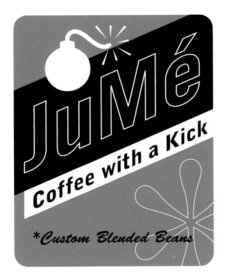

4

ORIGINAL CASUAL APPAREL FOR FENCERS

BiG
For Our
BRiTCHes™

ORIGINAL CASUAL APPAREL FOR FENCERS

Recipient

Distribution Location
30 THE FENWAY **BOSTON, MASSACHUSETTS 02215**

Contact
617.515.0955

Digital Location
www.big4ourbritches.com

S
M
L
XL

Since 2001

BIG FOR OUR BRITCHES

BIG FOR OUR BRITCHES

30 THE FENWAY **BOSTON, M**

1

2

3

1 **PUBLICIDAD GÓMEZ CHICA** | DESIGNER **SANTIAGO JARAMILLO** | CLIENT **LAS PALMAS RESTAURANT**
2 **SAYLES GRAPHIC DESIGN** | ART DIRECTOR **JOHN SAYLES** | CLIENT **PETALS DE PROVENCE**
3 **SAYLES GRAPHIC DESIGN** | DESIGNER **JOHN SAYLES** | CLIENT **NEPTUNE'S SEAGRILL**

1

2

1 **BE.DESIGN** | ART DIRECTOR **WILL BURKE** | DESIGNERS **ERIC READ, YUSUKE ASAKA, CORALIE RUSSO** | CLIENT **WORLDWISE, INC.**

2 **RE: SALZMAN DESIGNS** | ART DIRECTOR **IDA CHEINMAN** | DESIGNERS **IDA CHEINMAN, RICK SALZMAN** | CLIENT **LEE'S ICE CREAM**

FRONTIER ROOM

2203 First Avenue   Seattle Washington 98121
p 206/ 956-RIBS (7427)
Paul Michael, head chef   e frontierroom@seanet.com

FRONTIER ROOM

2203 First Avenue Seattle Washington 98121   p 206/ 956-RIBS (7427)   e frontierroom@seanet.com

RE: SALZMAN DESIGNS | ART DIRECTOR IDA CHEINMAN | DESIGNERS IDA CHEINMAN, RICK SALZMAN | CLIENT LITECAST

LITECAST

RE: SALZMAN DESIGNS | ART DIRECTOR IDA CHEINMAN | DESIGNERS IDA CHEINMAN, RICK SALZMAN | CLIENT LITECAST

1

2

1 **SAYLES GRAPHIC DESIGN** | ART DIRECTOR **JOHN SAYLES** | CLIENT **ISABELLA'S**
2 **SAYLES GRAPHIC DESIGN** | ART DIRECTOR **JOHN SAYLES** | CLIENT **PET KINGDOM**

1

2

3

4

1 **HG DESIGN** | DESIGNER **MATT PIERCE** | CLIENT **THUNDER EAGLE CYCLE SHOP**

2 **CFX CREATIVE** | ART DIRECTOR **CARLY H. FRANKLIN** | CLIENT **MEDBIZMARKET**

3 **GASKET** | ART DIRECTOR **MIKE CHRISTOFFEL** | CLIENT **GLAM**

4 **RICK JOHNSON & COMPANY** | DESIGNER **TIM MCGRATH** | CLIENT **CRUSTY UNDERWEAR**

Custodians of fine Australian wine

WOOL
LOO
MOO
WINES LOO

David Titsha
General Manager

Telephone +61 2 9252 0080
Facsimile +61 2 9252 8878

Woolloomooloo Wines
Royal Exchange PO Box R384
Sydney 1225 NSW
Australia

david@woolloomooloowines.com.au
www.woolloomooloowines.com.au

Custodians of fine Australian wine

WOOL
LOO
MOO
WINES LOO

WOOL
LOO
MOO
WINES LOO

ne Australian wine

Woolloomooloo
pron. wŏol-lŏo-mŏo-lŏo

The name Woolloomooloo is
steeped in indigenous Australian
[Aboriginal] heritage. The name
originally comes from 'Wulla Nulla'
meaning 'young male kangaroo'.

Telephone +61 2 9252 0080
Facsimile +61 2 9252 8878

Woolloomooloo Wines Pty Limited
Royal Exchange PO Box R384
Sydney 1225 NSW Australia

www.woolloomooloowines.com.au
ABN 26 080 837 084

John Olsen

EMERY VINCENT DESIGN | ART DIRECTOR **EMERY VINCENT DESIGN** | CLIENT **WOOLLOOMOOLOO WINES**

137

RETAIL, RESTAURANT, AND HOSPITALITY

1

EQUIFEMME
LIPOSOMAL PROGESTERONE CREAM

2

1 **CFX CREATIVE** | ART DIRECTOR **CARLY H. FRANKLIN** | CLIENT **WHEATLAND NATURALS**
2 **INOX DESIGN** | DESIGNER **ALESSANDRO FLORIDIA** | CLIENT **MR. GAO**

1

2

3

1 **ZIGZAG DESIGN** | ART DIRECTOR **RACHEL KARACA** | CLIENT **GROUNDED**

2 **MIAMI AD SCHOOL** | ART DIRECTOR **JONATHAN GOUTHIER** | DESIGNER **MIMI AWAMURA** | CLIENT **DOGMA GRILL**

3 **VRONTIKIS DESIGN OFFICE** | ART DIRECTOR **PETRULA VRONTIKIS** | DESIGNER **RON BLAYLOCK** | CLIENT **RED CAR WINE CO.**

1

SLAVE

2

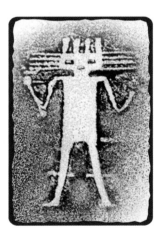

ATACAMA

1 **BE.DESIGN** | ART DIRECTOR **ERIC READ** | DESIGNER **DEBORAH SMITH READ** | CLIENT **SLAVE**
2 **BE.DESIGN** | ART DIRECTOR **ERIC READ** | DESIGNERS **ERIC READ, CORALIE RUSSO** | CLIENT **COST PLUS WORLD MARKET**

Harrods
KNIGHTSBRIDGE

URBAN RETREAT AT HARRODS
Fifth Floor, Harrods, Knightsbridge London SW1X 7XL Telephone 020 7893 8333 Fax 020 7893 8335
Registered in England No 2849316 VAT No 627575022 Registered Office Urban Retreats Limited 7 Munton Road London SE17 1PR

D. DESIGN | ART DIRECTOR **DEREK SAMUEL** | CLIENT **GEORGE HAMMER**

URBAN RETREAT

TIME SPACE COMFORT

URBAN RETREAT

Harrods

Harrods
KNIGHTSBRIDGE
URBAN RETREAT AT HARR...
Fifth Floor, Harrods, Knightsbridge London SW1X 7XL Telephor...
Registered in England No 2849316 VAT No 627575022 Registered Office Urb...

D. DESIGN | ART DIRECTOR **DEREK SAMUEL** | CLIENT **GEORGE HAMMER**

1 BAKKEN CREATIVE CO. | ART DIRECTOR MICHELLE BAKKEN | CLIENT FRASCATI RESTAURANT

2 BE.DESIGN | ART DIRECTOR WILL BURKE | DESIGNERS ERIC READ, DIANE HILDE | CLIENT COST PLUS WORLD MARKET

3 METZLER ASSOCIATES | ART DIRECTOR MARC-ANTOINE HERRMANN | DESIGNER JEAN-RENEE GUEGAN | CLIENT SCAPPUCCI

2433 BOONE AVE VENICE CA 90291

tel 310 600 0144 fax 310 827 7367

www.dishcatering.com

2433 BOONE AVE VENICE CA 90291

tel 310 600 0144 fax 310 827 7367

www.dishcatering.com

SPECIAL MODERN DESIGN | ART DIRECTOR **KARN BARRANCO** | CLIENT **DISH CATERING**

1

BUZZ BUILDING MAINTENANCE

2

3

Sukita®

1 **INSIGHT DESIGN COMMUNICATIONS** | ART DIRECTOR **TRACY HOLDMAN** | DESIGNER **LEAH CARMICHAEL** | CLIENT **BUZZ BUILDING MAINTENANCE**

2 **BE.DESIGN** | ART DIRECTOR **ERIC READ** | DESIGNER **DEBORAH SMITH READ** | CLIENT **KARMA CREATIONS**

3 **DIL BRANDS** | ART DIRECTOR **NORIVAL MARTINS** | CLIENT **AMBEV**

D. DESIGN | ART DIRECTOR DEREK SAMUEL | CLIENT GEORGE HAMMER

1

2

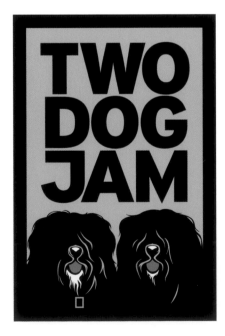

1 **KNEZIC/PAVONE** | ART DIRECTOR **ROBINSON C. SMITH** | CLIENT **COOL FAITH APPAREL**
2 **KNEZIC/PAVONE** | ART DIRECTOR **ROBINSON C. SMITH** | CLIENT **STONE COTTAGE PRESERVES**

zigzag design
4006 oak #3
kansas city, mo 64111

816 213 1198
raka@uzigzag.com
uzigzag.com

zig
zag

☐ invoice
☐ proposal
☐ estimate
☐ thank you
☐ brilliant idea
☐ gossip
☐ apology
☐ favor
☐ other: _____

rachel karaca

zigzag design
4006 oak #3
kansas city, mo 64111

816 213 1198
raka@uzigzag.com
uzigzag.com

zig
zag

zigzag design
4006 oak #3
kansas city, mo 64111

816 213 1198
raka@uzigzag.com
uzigzag.com

zig
zag

zigzag design
4006 oak #3
kansas city, mo 64111

816 213 1198
raka@uzigzag.com
uzigzag.com

zig
zag

Dear _____,
            Name Thankee

This is just a(n) _____ note to say thank you for _____.
                  Insert adjective   Insert reason

Your (check all that apply) ☐ kindness   means a great deal to me. Thanks again for being so _____.
                           ☐ genius   Insert adjective
                           ☐ love
                           ☐ friendship
                           ☐ humor
                           ☐ pleasant nature
                           ☐ talent
                           ☐ understanding
                           ☐ opinion

Sincerely,

_____
            Thanker sign here

1

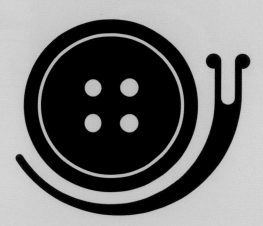

2

1 **ROBERT FROEDGE DESIGN** | ART DIRECTOR **ROBERT FROEDGE** | CLIENT **SNIPS & SNAILS**

2 **ROBERT FROEDGE DESIGN** | ART DIRECTOR **ROBERT FROEDGE** | CLIENT **NELLIE'S ORIGINALS**

fleurs

FLORAL DESIGN FAR FROM ORDINARY
FRESH, VIBRANT FLOWERS
GIFT BASKETS
GOURMET FOODS
SPECIALTY WINES & CHOCOLATES
CORPORATE • WEDDINGS • FUNERALS

The Forum, Mar
Blenheim
Tel/Fax 03 577
Freephone 0800
Email: flowers@fleu

FLORAL DESIGN FAR FROM ORDINARY

CARE GUIDE

WWW.fleurs.net.nz

fleurs

Kimberley Judd

The Forum, Market Place
Blenheim
Tel/Fax 03 577 9433
Freephone 0800 11 5599
Email: flowers@fleurs.net.nz

EDUCATION, HEALTH, AND NONPROFIT

1

2

THE UNITED STATES
CONFERENCE OF MAYORS

CANCER AWARENESS PROGRAM

1 **LEWIS COMMUNICATIONS** | ART DIRECTOR **ROBERT FROEDGE** | CLIENT **FLORIDA'S GREAT NORTHWEST**

2 **HAMBLY & WOOLLEY** | CLIENT **U.S. CONFERENCE OF MAYORS**

THE INSTITUTE OF CONTEMPORARY ART

955 BOYLSTON BOSTON MASSACHUSETTS 02115 USA · WWW.ICABOSTON.ORG · FAX 617.266.4021 PHONE 617.266.5152

THE INSTITUTE OF CONTEMPORARY ART

955 BOYLSTON BOSTON MASSACHUSETTS 02115 USA WWW.ICABOSTON.ORG FAX 617.266.4021 PHONE 617.266.5152

ICA

ELIZABETH JESSNER
DEVELOPMENT ASSISTANT

617.927.6603

JESSNER@ICABOSTON.ORG

THE INSTITUTE OF CONTEMPORARY ART

955 BOYLSTON B

1

CAVION™
CARE MANAGEMENT SYSTEM

2

Friends
for
Sight
Your vision is our focus.

3

eTM
Entitat de Transport Metropolità

4

1 **BECKER DESIGN** | DESIGNER **NEIL BECKER** | CLIENT **CAVION**

2 **LOVE COMMUNICATIONS** | ART DIRECTOR **PRESTON WOOD** | DESIGNERS **CRAIG LEE, PRESTON WOOD** | CLIENT **CRAIG LEE**

3 **PEPE GIMENO—PROYECTO GRAFICO/ESTUDIO PACO BASCUNAN** | ART DIRECTORS **PEPE GIMENO, PACO BASCUNAN** | DESIGNERS **PEPE GIMENO, PACO BASCUNAN,** **DIDAC BALLESTER** | CLIENT **ENTITAT DE TRANSPORTS METROPOLITAN DE VALENCIA**

4 **WAVE 3** | DESIGNER **RHONDA HARSHFIELD** | CLIENT **LOUISVILLE REALTORS.COM**

1

2

1 **KNEZIC/PAVONE** | ART DIRECTOR **ROBINSON C. SMITH** | CLIENT **PENNSYLVANIA COALITION AGAINST RAPE**
2 **LOVE COMMUNICATIONS** | ART DIRECTOR **PRESTON WOOD** | DESIGNER **CRAIG LEE** | CLIENT **CRAIG LEE**

the cloud foundation

the cloud foundation

the cloud foundation

cloud place
647 boylston street   boston   massachusetts 02116
www.cloudfoundation.org
phone 617.262.2949   fax 617.262.2848

email info@cloudfoundation.org   www.cloudfoundation.org

cloud place   647 boylston street   boston massachusetts 02116   phone 617.262.2949   fax 617.262.2848

PLUS DESIGN INC. | ART DIRECTOR ANITA MEYER | DESIGNERS ANITA MEYER, VIVIAN LAW | CLIENT THE CLOUD FOUNDATION

1

2

3

1 **DUO DESIGN** | DESIGNERS **VALTERS LINDBERGS, EMMANUELLE BECKER** | CLIENT **FRANCE TELECOM FORMATION**

2 **LEAGAS DELANEY SF** | DESIGNER **EMILIA FILIPOI** | CLIENT **STEP UP NETWORK**

3 **HONEY DESIGN** | ART DIRECTOR **ROBIN HONEY** | DESIGNER **JASON RECKER** | CLIENT **CALLAGHAN CONSULTING**

1

creative**adoptions**

2

3

1 FRESHBRAND, INC. | ART DIRECTOR MARCEL VENTER | CLIENT CREATIVE ADOPTIONS

2 GOTT FOLK MCCANN-ERIKSON | ART DIRECTOR EINRA GYLFAYSON | CLIENT MENNT.IS

3 ALR DESIGN | ART DIRECTOR NOAH SCALIN | CLIENT ABC NO RIO

URBAN HABITAT

URBAN HABITAT

JULIET ELLIS
EXECUTIVE DIRECTOR

436 14TH STREET, STE 1205
OAKLAND, CA 94612
T 510 839 9512 F 510 839 9610
jre@urbanhabitat.org
www.urbanhabitat.org

URBAN HABITAT

436 14TH STREET, STE 1205
OAKLAND, CA 94612

436 14TH STREET, STE 1205   OAKLAND, CA 94612
T 510 839 9510 F 510 839 9610
www.urbanhabitat.org

critical **support**

OUR HOSPITAL, OUR FUTURE

critical **support**

OUR HOSPITAL, OUR FUTURE

Oakville-Trafalgar Memorial Hospital Charitable Corporation

Ian Cockwell
CAMPAIGN CO-CHAIR
campaign@haltonhealthcare.on.ca

Critical Support   327 Reynolds Street   TEL 905.338.4465
Oakville, Ontario L6J 3L7   FAX 905.338.4135

Oakville-Trafalgar Memorial Hospital Charitable Corporation
327 Reynolds Street, Oakville, Ontario L6J 3L7
TEL 905.338.4465 FAX 905.338.4135
EMAIL campaign@haltonhealthcare.on.ca

THE RIORDON DESIGN GROUP | ART DIRECTOR DAN WHEATON | DESIGNER ALAN KPPAN | CLIENT OAKVILLE-TRAFALGAR MEMORIAL HOSPITAL

1

National
Cancer Institute
of Canada

2

1 **HAMBLY & WOOLLEY** | ART DIRECTOR **BARB WOOLLEY** | DESIGNER **DOMINIC AYRE** | CLIENT **NATIONAL CANCER INSTITUTE OF CANADA**
2 **SAYLES GRAPHIC DESIGN** | ART DIRECTOR **JOHN SAYLES** | CLIENT **METRO ARTS ALLIANCE**

1

CulinarySchool
OF LONDON

2

1 **HONEY DESIGN** | ART DIRECTOR **ROBIN HONEY** | DESIGNER **JASON RECKER** | CLIENT **CULINARY SCHOOL OF LONDON**
2 **MORRIS CREATIVE INC.** | ART DIRECTOR **STEVEN MORRIS** | CLIENT **MONARCH HOMELESS HIGH SCHOOL**

CUBITT
Gallery and Studios
8 Angel Mews
London N1 9HH
T +44 (0)20 7278 8226
F +44 (0)20 7278 2544
E info@cubittartists.org.uk
www.cubittartists.org.uk

Cubitt Artists Limited
Company Limited by Guarantee
Registered in England and Wales No. 2748649
Registered Charity No. 1049653
Registered Office 315 — 317 Ballards Lane, London N12 8LY

RECREATION AND ENTERTAINMENT

1

A WORLDSPACE CHANNEL

2

1 FUSZION COLLABORATIVE | ART DIRECTOR RICHARD LEE HEFFNER | DESIGNER CHRISTIAN BALDO | CLIENT WORLDSPACE
2 UP DESIGN BUREAU | ART DIRECTOR TRAVIS BROWN | CLIENT RICHMOND RACEWAY

1

2

3

4

5

1 **LSD** | ART DIRECTOR **LAURENCE STEVENS** | DESIGNER **LAURENCE STEVENS** | CLIENT LAURENCE STEVENS DESIGN
2 **LSD** | ART DIRECTOR **LAURENCE STEVENS** | DESIGNER **LAURENCE STEVENS** | CLIENT SONY MUSIC
3 **LSD** | ART DIRECTOR **LAURENCE STEVENS** | DESIGNER **LAURENCE STEVENS** | CLIENT C2 MUSIC MANAGEMENT
4 **LSD** | ART DIRECTOR **LAURENCE STEVENS** | DESIGNER **LAURENCE STEVENS** | CLIENT POLYDOR RECORDS UK
5 **LSD** | ART DIRECTOR **LAURENCE STEVENS** | DESIGNER **LAURENCE STEVENS** | CLIENT DAVE STEWART

i.v. records

1701 CHURCH STREET NASHVILLE TN 37203 PHO: 615.320.1444 FAX: 615.320.0750 WEB: WWW.IVRECORDS.COM

i.v. records

JEREMY BOSE writer/producer
1701 CHURCH STREET NASHVILLE TN 37203 PHO: 615.320.1444 FAX: 615.320.0750
WEB: WWW.IVRECORDS.COM E-MAIL: JBOSE@IVRECORDS.COM

LEWIS COMMUNICATIONS | ART DIRECTOR ROBERT GROEDGE | CLIENT WHISTLER'S ENTERTAINMENT GROUP

EAST TOWER

SOUTH TOWER

NORTH TOWER

GOTTSCHALK + ASH INTERNATIONAL | ART DIRECTOR **STUART ASH** | DESIGNER **SONJA CHOW** | CLIENT **BELL MOBILITY OFFICES**

1

2

1

2

3

1 **CHASE DESIGN GROUP** | ART DIRECTOR **MARGO CHASE** | CLIENT **CHER**
2 **TORNADO DESIGN** | ART DIRECTORS **AL QUATTROCCTTI, JEFF SMITH** | CLIENT **MOCEAN**
3 **TORNADO DESIGN** | ART DIRECTORS **AL QUATTROCCTTI, JEFF SMITH** | CLIENT **HBO**

LITTLE EGG CHARTERS

Light Line and Fly Fishing Guide Service

LITTLE EGG CHARTER

Light Line and Fly Fishing Guide Service

Capt. Christian Handel • Little Egg Harbor, NJ • 609-8

1

BUENOS AIRES PASTRIES

2

3

1 ROKFIL DESIGN | ART DIRECTOR MARIANA B. PABON | CLIENT BUENOS AIRES PASTRIES
2 I. PARIS DESIGN | ART DIRECTOR ISAAC PARIS | CLIENT AMERICAN DANCE THEATER
3 SAYLES GRAPHIC DESIGN | ART DIRECTOR JOHN SAYLES | CLIENT JOHNNY NIGHT TRAIN

1

2

3

4

5

1 **DIGITAL SOUP** | ART DIRECTOR **PASH** | CLIENT **EUNIVERSE**

2 **MONSTER DESIGN** | ART DIRECTORS **HANNAH WYGAL, THERESA VERANTH** | DESIGNER **DENISE SAKAKI** | CLIENT **MOXFOX**

3 **MORRIS CREATIVE INC.** | ART DIRECTOR **STEVEN MORRIS** | CLIENT **LOLO COMPANY**

4 **DIGITAL SOUP** | ART DIRECTOR **PASH** | DESIGNERS **BILL BARMINSKI & PASH** | CLIENT **BRASH/ESSENTIAL ENTERTAINMENT**

5 **IRIDIUM, A DESIGN AGENCY** | ART DIRECTOR **JEAN-LUC DENAT** | DESIGNERS **JEAN-LUC DENAT, ETIENNE DESSETTE** | CLIENT **LES ECRITS DES HAUTES—TERRES**

1

2

3

1 **I. PARIS DESIGN** | ART DIRECTOR **ISAAC PARIS** | CLIENT **RECORD TIME LABEL**
2 **PACEY + PACEY** | ART DIRECTOR **ROBERT PACEY** | DESIGNER **MICHAEL PACEY** | CLIENT **VANCOUVER DART ASSOC.**
3 **SAGMEISTER INC.** | ART DIRECTOR **STEFAN SAGMEISTER** | DESIGNER **MATHIAS ERNSTBERGER** | CLIENT **LOU REED**

KOLÉGRAM DESIGN | ART DIRECTOR **MIKE TEIXEIRA** | CLIENT **THÉÂTRE DU TRILLIUM**

1

Jup

2

3

1 **LSD** | ART DIRECTOR **LAURENCE STEVENS** | DESIGNER **LAURENCE STEVENS** | CLIENT **ARTIST NETWORK RECORDS**
2 **TORNADO DESIGN** | ART DIRECTORS **AL QUATTROCCTTI, JEFF SMITH** | CLIENT **ROCKET STUDIO**
3 **BE.DESIGN** | ART DIRECTOR **WILL BURKE** | DESIGNERS **ERIC READ, YUSUKE ASAKA** | CLIENT **MICROSOFT**

MISCELLANEOUS

THE Parlor

BECKER DESIGN | ART DIRECTOR **NEIL BECKER** | DESIGNER **SARAH FRITZ** | CLIENT **THE PARLOR**

THE

Parlor

ANN WEBER
PROPRIETOR

W161 N11629 CHURCH ST. GERMANTOWN, WI 53022
P 262 253.6800 F 262 253.0068 theparlorsalon@hotmail.com

THE

Parlor

W161 N11629 CHURCH ST. GERMANTOWN, WI 53022 P 262 253.680

THE

Parlor

W161 N11629 CHURCH ST. GERMANTOWN, WI 53022

BECKER DESIGN | ART DIRECTOR NEIL BECKER | DESIGNER SARAH FRITZ | CLIENT THE PARLOR

1

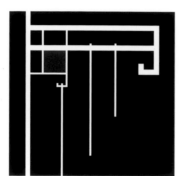

2

WRIGHT
AT HOME
LLC

1 **DESIGN GUYS** | ART DIRECTOR **STEVEN SIKORA** | DESIGNER **JOHN MOES** | CLIENT **DESIGN GUYS**
2 **DESIGN GUYS** | ART DIRECTOR **STEVEN SIKORA** | DESIGNER **JOHN MOES** | CLIENT **DESIGN GUYS**

BULLDOG DRUMMOND | ART DIRECTOR **NEIL BELLEFEVILLE** | DESIGNER **HEIDI ARRIZABALAGA** | CLIENT **BULLDOG DRUMMOND**

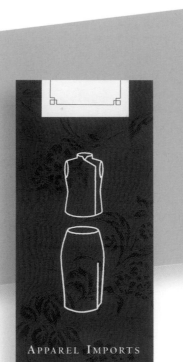

馬

ANNA LEE

001 415 794 1220

ANNAYINGLEE@AOL.COM

ANNA LEE

APPAREL IMPORTS

APPAREL IMPORTS

1

Creative *fire*

2

DOORS OPEN
TORONTO

1 IN-HOUSE (CREATIVE FIRE) | ART DIRECTOR HEATHER McKENDRY | DESIGNER HEATHER McKENDRY | CLIENT CREATIVE FIRE

2 REACTOR ART + DESIGN | DESIGNERS SHARI SPIER, JAMES TURNER | CLIENT HERITAGE TORONTO

PENTAVARIT

2712 LARMON DR., NASHVILLE, TN 37204 > PHONE: 615.269.6543 > FAX: 615.269.6849 > PENTAVARIT.COM

PENTAVARIT

PAUL EVANS

2712 LARMON DR., NASHVILLE, TN 37204 > PHONE: 615.269.6543
FAX: 615.269.6849 > pevans@pentavarit.com > PENTAVARIT.COM

2712 LARMON DR., NASHVILLE, TN 37204

PENTAVARIT

2712 LARMON DR., NASHVILLE, TN 37204 > PHONE: 615.269.6543

PENTAVARIT

1

cherry pie

2 **YES**

YOUR ELECTRICAL SUPPLY SOURCE

3 **PAWS**

Play, adventure and walking services for your dog.

1 **DIGITAL SOUP** | ART DIRECTOR **PASH** | CLIENT **CHERRY PIE**
2 **WAVE 3** | DESIGNER **RHONDA HARSHFIELD**
3 **BAKKEN CREATIVE CO.** | ART DIRECTOR **MICHELLE BAKKEN** | CLIENT **PAWS**

1

2

1 **DESIGN GUYS** | ART DIRECTOR **STEVEN SIKORA** | DESIGNER **ANNE PETERSON** | CLIENT **ANDRA PATZOLDT**

2 **MORRIS CREATIVE INC.** | ART DIRECTOR **STEVEN MORRIS** | DESIGNER **DEANNE WILLIAMSON** | CLIENT **WATTERS & WATTERS**

YOUR LIST   25 HAMPSTEAD LANE   TEL 0208 347 7816   WWW.YOURLISTLTD.COM
             LONDON N6 4RT   FAX 0208 342 8848   INFO@YOURLISTLTD.COM

REGISTERED NO: 4297981 REGISTERED OFFICE: 205/207 CRESCENT ROAD NEW BARNET HERTS EN4 8SB

NB STUDIO | ART DIRECTORS NICK FINNEY, ALAN DYE, BEN STOTT | DESIGNER NICK VINCENT | CLIENT YOUR LIST

STUDENT WORK | ART DIRECTOR RACHEL KARACA | CLIENT CURIOUS MINDS IDENTITY

1   abc²

2   lighthouse

3   intellivoice

1 **HAMBLY & WOOLLEY** | ART DIRECTOR **BARB WOOLLEY** | DESIGNER **DOMINIC AYRE** | CLIENT **ABC2**
2 **WILSON HARVEY** | ART DIRECTOR **PAUL BURGESS** | DESIGNER **RICHARD BAKER** | CLIENT **LIGHTHOUSE**
3 **WILSON HARVEY** | ART DIRECTOR **PAUL BURGESS** | DESIGNER **DANIEL ELLIOTT** | CLIENT **INTELLIVOICE**

NORAC

IMPORT-EXPORT

4405, rue Lafrance
Montréal (Québec) Canada
H2A 2G1
Tél. :   (514) 951-9412
Téléc. : (514) 529-8051
Courriel : caronmichel@yahoo.ca

4405 Lafrance Street
Montreal, Quebec, Canada
H2A 2G1
Tel. :   (514) 951-9412
Fax :   (514) 529-8051
E-mail: caronmichel@yahoo.ca

NORAC

T R A D E R S

Michel Caron
President

BEAULIEU CONCEPTS GRAPHIQUES INC. | ART DIRECTOR GILLES BEAULIEU | CLIENT NORAC IMPORT-EXPORT

CARA SANDERS visuals
425 586 4964   cara_sanders@toplinecorp.com

13150 SE 32nd Street   Bellevue WA 98005
   425 643 3003   425 643 3846   **TOPLINE**

TOPLINE

TOPLINE
13150 SE 32nd Street
Bellevue WA   98005

13150 SE 32nd Street   Bellevue WA   98005   **T** 425 643 3003   **F** 425 643 3846

THE TOPLINE CORPORATION | ART DIRECTOR HAREL WALDMAN | DESIGNER CARA SANDERS | CLIENT THE TOPLINE CORPORATION

1

2

3

1 **WILSON HARVEY** | ART DIRECTOR **PAUL BURGESS** | CLIENT **ROUTE ONE**
2 **BECKER DESIGN** | DESIGNER **NEIL BECKER** | CLIENT **REDI HELP**
3 **WILSON HARVEY** | ART DIRECTOR **PAUL BURGESS** | DESIGNER **DANIEL ELLIOTT** | CLIENT **DRAKES GROUP**

1 metrocube³

2 NM@F

new mexico's advertising voice

1 **WILSON HARVEY** | ART DIRECTOR **PAUL BURGESS** | CLIENT **METROCUBE**
2 **RICK JOHNSON & COMPANY** | DESIGNER **TIM McGRATH** | CLIENT **NEW MEXICO AD FED**

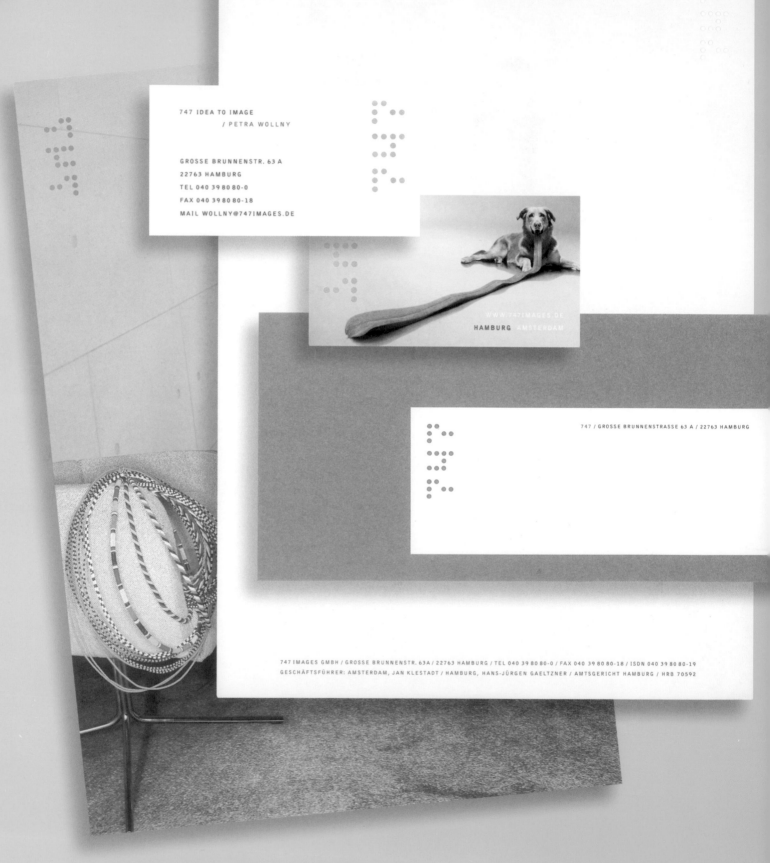

747 IDEA TO IMAGE   HAMBURG AMSTERDAM   WWW.747IMAGES.DE

747 IDEA TO IMAGE
/ PETRA WOLLNY

GROSSE BRUNNENSTR. 63 A
22763 HAMBURG
TEL 040 39 80 80-0
FAX 040 39 80 80-18
MAIL WOLLNY@747IMAGES.DE

WWW.747IMAGES.DE
HAMBURG AMSTERDAM

747 / GROSSE BRUNNENSTRASSE 63 A / 22763 HAMBURG

747 IMAGES GMBH / GROSSE BRUNNENSTR. 63A / 22763 HAMBURG / TEL 040 39 80 80-0 / FAX 040 39 80 80-18 / ISDN 040 39 80 80-19
GESCHÄFTSFÜHRER: AMSTERDAM, JAN KLESTADT / HAMBURG, HANS-JÜRGEN GAELTZNER / AMTSGERICHT HAMBURG / HRB 70592

FORMAT DESIGN | DESIGNER **KNUT ETTLING** | CLIENT **747 IMAGES**

1

2

KINGSLEY
KARDS

1 **IRIDIUM, A DESIGN AGENCY** | ART DIRECTOR **MARIO L'ECUYER** | CLIENT **CANADIAN RESEARCH CHAIRS**
2 **MORRIS CREATIVE INC.** | ART DIRECTOR **STEVEN MORRIS** | CLIENT **KINGSLEY KARDS**

Communications & Marketing
from the Ground Up

262 Willow Street
second floor
New Haven, CT 06511

(203) 785–8262
www.grassroots-llc.com

www.grassroots-llc.com

Communications & Marketing
from the Ground Up

Elise Annes
262 Willow Street
second floor

New Haven, CT 06511
(203) 785–8262
elise@grassroots-llc.com

Communications & Marketing
from the Ground Up

Communications & Marketing
from the Ground Up

262 Willow Street
second floor
New Haven, CT 06511
(203) 785–8262
www.grassroots-llc.com

Grassroots

Grassroots

Grassroots

Grassroots

ICEHOUSE DESIGN | ART DIRECTOR BJORN AKSELSEN | CLIENT GRASSROOTS

1

jade

2

ajm

1

2 □: THE LAUNCHPAD

1 **MONDERER DESIGN** | ART DIRECTOR **STUART MONDERER** | DESIGNER **JEFFREY GOBIN** | CLIENT **SOCKEYE NETWORKS**
2 **WILSON HARVEY** | ART DIRECTOR **PAUL BURGESS** | CLIENT **THE LAUNCHPAD**

Archer Street

Frank Cottrell Boyce

Archer Street

Studio 5, 10-11 Archer Street
London W1V 7HG
tel. +44 (0)20 7439 0540
fax. +44 (0)20 7437 1182
email. frank@archerstreet.com

with compliments

Archer Street

Studio 5, 10-11 Archer Street
London W1V 7HG
tel. +44 (0)20 7439 0540
fax. +44 (0)20 7437 1182
email. films@archerstreet.com

Archer Street Limited
Studio 5, 10-11 Archer Street
London W1V 7HG
tel. +44 (0)20 7439 0540
fax. +44 (0)20 7437 1182
email. films@archerstreet.com

Directors: Andy Paterson
Frank Cottrell Boyce   Anand Tucker

Company Registered No. 3537276

Registered Address:
10 Orange Street, London WC2H 7DQ

1

2

1 EMMA WILSON DESIGN CO. | DESIGNER EMMA WILSON | CLIENT EMMA WILSON DESIGN CO.
2 EMMA WILSON DESIGN CO. | DESIGNER EMMA WILSON | CLIENT EMMA WILSON DESIGN CO.

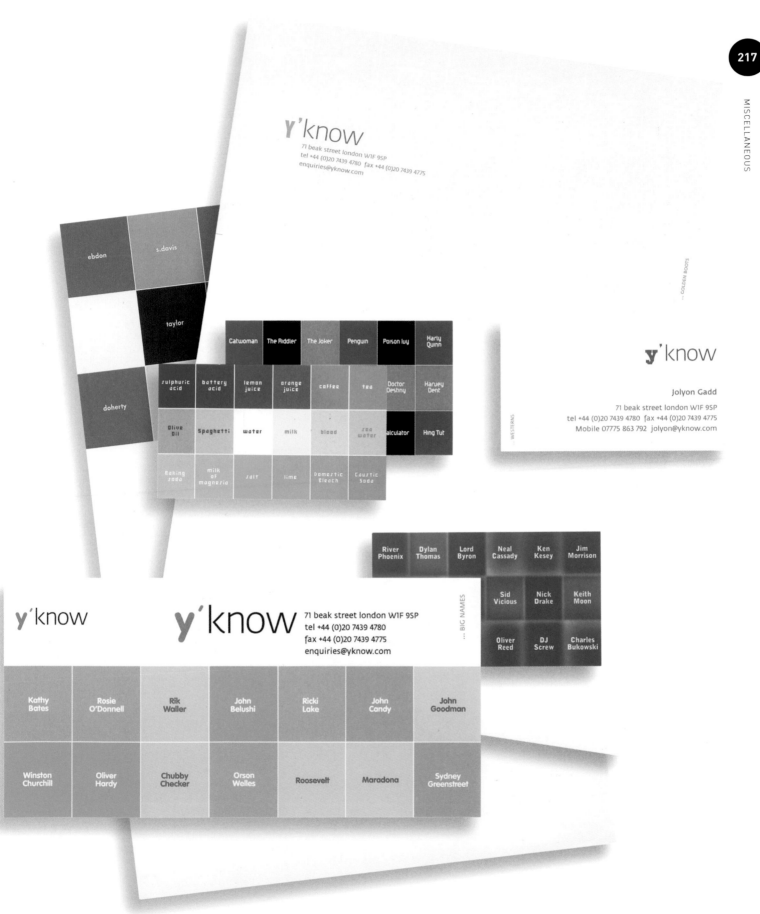

— GOLDEN BOOTS

WESTERNS

... BIG NAMES

HOME PACKAGE DELIVERY BOX

1 **CITY OF KITCHENER** | ART DIRECTOR **JOLENE MacDONALD** | CLIENT **CIRCA DEVELOPMENT**

2 **HG DESIGN** | ART DIRECTOR **STEVE COOPER** | CLIENT **BOBBYBOX**

3 **SAYLES GRAPHIC DESIGN** | ART DIRECTOR **JOHN SAYLES** | CLIENT **MOORE FAMILY**

4 **SAYLES GRAPHIC DESIGN** | ART DIRECTOR **JOHN SAYLES** | CLIENT **SAYLES GRAPHIC DESIGN**

1

westone
PLASTIC AND COSMETIC SURGERY

2

riskcapitalpartners

3

ellisknox
PRODUCT INNOVATION

1 WILSON HARVEY | ART DIRECTOR PAUL BURGESS | DESIGNER DANIEL ELLIOTT | CLIENT WEST ONE PLASTIC SURGEONS
2 WILSON HARVEY | ART DIRECTOR PAUL BURGESS | DESIGNER DANIEL ELLIOTT | CLIENT RISK CAPITAL PARTNERS
3 WILSON HARVEY | ART DIRECTOR PAUL BURGESS | DESIGNER STEPHANIE HARRISON | CLIENT ELLIS KNOX

charlotte sanderson (dip.ISD) garden & landscape design

23 coldstream gardens london SW18 1LJ **t/f** 020 8877 9167 **m** 07748 651 653
e charlotte@sandersongardendesign.com **i** www.sandersongardendesign.com

charlotte sanderson (dip.ISD)
garden & landscape design

23 coldstream gardens london SW18 1LJ
t/f 020 8877 9167 **m** 07748 651 653
e charlotte@sandersongardendesign.com
i www.sandersongardendesign.com

DIRECTORY

178 AARDIGE ONTWEPERS
Amsterdam, Netherlands
info@178aardigeontwepers.nl

A2-GRAPHICS/SW/HK
London, United Kingdom
info@a2-graphics.co.uk

AFTERHOURS GROUP
Jakarta, Indonesia
brahm@afterhoursgroup.com

ALR DESIGN
Richmond, VA, USA
noah@alrdesign.com

ANGRY PORCUPINE DESIGN
Cupertino, CA, USA
cheryl@angryporcupine.com

A PLUS B
New York, NY, USA
ab_alx@yahoo.com

ATELIER TADEUSZ PIECHURA
Lodz, Poland
jjw@uni-film.pl

BAKKEN CREATIVE CO.
Berkeley, CA, USA
mbakken@bakkencreativeco.com

BALANCE DESIGN
Greenwich, CT, USA
carey@balancedesign.net

BE.DESIGN
San Rafael, CA, USA
shinichi_eguchi@beplanet.com

BEAULIEU CONCEPTS GRAPHIQUES INC.
Candiac, Quebec, Canada
bcg@videotron.ca

BECKER DESIGN
Milwaukee, WI, USA
neil@beckerdesign.net

BENCIUM
Budapest, Hungary
csbence@bencium.hu

BULLDOG DRUMMOND
San Diego, CA, USA
catharine@bulldogdrummond.com

BURD & PATTERSON
W. Des Moines, IA, USA

CAHAN AND ASSOCIATES
San Francisco, CA, USA
info@cahanassociates.com

CAHOOTS
Boston, MA, USA
carol@cahootsdesign.com

CATO PURNELL PARTNERS
Richmond, Victoria, Australia
melbourne@cato.com.au

CDT DESIGN
London, United Kingdom
stuart@cdt-design.co.uk

CHASE DESIGN GROUP
Los Angeles, CA, USA
husam@chasedesigngroup.com

CHEN DESIGN ASSOCIATES
San Francisco, CA, USA
info@chendesign.com

CFX CREATIVE
Bellingham, WA, USA
info@cfxcreative.com

CITY OF KITCHENER
Kitchener ON, Canada
terry.marr@city.kitchener.on.ca

CPD
Melbourne, Victotia, Australia
d.ohehir@cpdtotal.com.au

CREATIVE FIRE
Bellingham, WA, USA
hmckendry@earthlink.net

D. DESIGN
London, United Kingdom
dereksamuel@virgin.net

DANIEL ELLIOTT
London, United Kingdom
delliott@hotmail.com

DESIGN GUYS
Minneapolis, MN, USA
info@designguys.com

DEW GIBBONS
London, United Kingdom
caty@dewgibbons.com

DIGITAL DESIGN WORKS
Gladwyne, PA, USA
mbugler@ddwinc.com

DIGITAL SOUP
Culver City, CA, USA
pash@digitalsoup.com

DIECKS GROUP
New York, NY, USA
claire@diecks.com

DIL BRANDS
São Paulo, Brazil
dilpackdesign@dil.com.br

DUCKS DESIGN, HAMBURG
Hamburg, Germany
contact@duckdesign.de

DUO DESIGN
Charenton-le-pont, France
duodesign@wanadoo.fr

EMERY VINCENT DESIGN
Surrey Hills, Sydney, Australia
sharon.nixon@emeryvincentdesign.com

EMI FILM AND TV
Los Angeles, CA, USA
michelle.azzopardi@emicap.com

EMMA WILSON DESIGN CO.
Seattle, WA, USA
emma@emmadesignco.com

ENERGY ENERGY DESIGN
Los Gatos, CA, USA
lesleyg@nrgdesign.com

ENTERPRISE IG
Tokyo, Japan
hidetaka.matsunaga@enterpriseig.com

FIREBOX MEDIA
San Francisco, CA, USA
audrey@fireboxmedia.com

FORMAT DESIGN
Hamburg, Germany
ettling@format.hh.com

FRESHBRAND, INC.
Denver, CO, USA
marcel@freshbrand.com

FUSZION COLLABORATIVE
Alexandria, VA, USA
john@fusion.com

GARY BASEMAN
Los Angeles, CA, USA
basemanart@earthlink.net

GASKET
Paddington, Brisbane, Australia
plazma@gil.com.av

GILLESPIE DESIGN, INC.
New York, NY, USA
maureen@gillespiedesign.com

GINGER BEE CREATIVE
Helena, MT, USA
gingerbee@qwest.net

GOTT FOLK McCANN-ERICKSON
Reykjavic, Iceland
einar@gottfolk.is

GOTTSCHALK + ASH INTERNATIONAL
Toronto, ON, Canada
info@gplusa.com

GRAPHISCHE FORMGEBUNG
Bochum, Germany
Herbert.rohsiepe@gelsen.net

GUNNAR SWANSON DESIGN OFFICE
Ventura, CA, USA
gunnar@gunnarswanson.com

GWEN FRANCIS DESIGN GROUP
Cupertino, CA, USA

HAMBLY & WOOLLEY
Toronto, ON, Canada
bobh@hamblywoolley.com

HAT-TRICK DESIGN
London, United Kingdom
jamie@hat-trickdesign.co.uk

HEAD QUARTER
Mainz, Germany
head@headquater.com

HG DESIGN
Wichita, KS, USA
scooper@hgdesign.com

HINGE
Chantilly, VA, USA
doug@studiohinge.com

HONEY DESIGN
London, ON, Canada
jason@honey.on.ca

I PARIS DESIGN
Brooklyn, NY, USA
iparisdgn@gis.net

ICEHOUSE DESIGN
New Haven, CT, USA
bjoran.akselsen@snet.net

IDEOGRAMA
Cuernavac, Morocco, Mexico
pep@ideograma.com

IMAGINE THAT DESIGN STUDIO
San Francisco, CA, USA
doit@imaginethatsf.com

INOX DESIGN
Milan, Italy
mauro@inoxdesign.it

INSIGHT DESIGN COMMUNICATIONS
Wichita, KS, USA
tracy@idcweb.net

IRIDIUM, A DESIGN COMPANY
Ottawa, ON, Canada
mario@iridium192.com

JANE CAMERON DESIGN
Adelaide, SA, Australia
jcd@adelaide.on.net

KARIZMA CULTURE
Vancouver, Canada
perryc@telus.net

KNEZIC/PAVONE
Harrisburg, PA, USA
rsmith@kpadv.net

KOLÉGRAM DESIGN
Hull, QC, Canada
mike@kolegram.com

LAURENCE STEVENS DESIGN (LSD)
London, England, UK
info@lsdvision.co.uk

LAVA GRAPHIC DESIGNERS
Netherlands
fieke@lava.nl

LE-PALMIER
Hamburg, Germany
design@lepalmiev.de

LEAGAS DELANEY SF
San Francisco, CA, USA
amelia.filipoi@leagassf.com

LEMLEY DESIGN CO.
Seattle, WA, USA
david@lemleydesign.com

LEWIS COMMUNICATIONS
Nashville, TN, USA
robert@lewiscommunications.com

LISKA + ASSOCIATES
Chicago, IL, USA
agray@liska.com

**LLOYD'S GRAPHIC DESIGN
AND COMMUNICATION**
Belenheim, New Zealand
lloydgraphics@xtra.co.nz

LOVE COMMUNICATIONS
Salt Lake City, UT, USA
pwood@lovecomm.net

MALIK DESIGN
South Amboy, NJ, USA
kilam@optonline.net

MARIUS FAHRNER DESIGN
Hamburg, Germany
marius@formgefuehl.de

METHOD
San Francisco, CA, USA
patrick@method.com

METZLER & ASSOCIATES
Paris, France
maherrmann@metzler.fr

MIASO DESIGN
Chicago, IL, USA
kristin@miasodesign.com

**MICHAEL POWELL DESIGN &
ART DIRECTION**
Memphis, TN, USA
mpowell6@midsouth.rr.com

MIAMI AD SCHOOL
Miami Beach, FLUSA

ML DESIGN
Los Angeles, CA, USA
marielafa@earthlink.net

MONDERER DESIGN
Cambridge, MA, USA
stewart@monderer.com

MONSTER DESIGN
Redmond, WA, USA
denise@monsterinvasion.com

MORRIS CREATIVE, INC.
San Diego, CA, USA
aimme@thinkfeelwork.com

MORTENSEN DESIGN
Mountain View, CA, USA
gmort@mortdes.com

MUCCA DESIGN
New York, NY, USA
christine.celic@muccadesign.com

NASSAR DESIGN
Brookline, MA, USA
n.nassar@verizon.net

NB STUDIO
London, United Kingdom
mail@nbstudio.co.uk

NESNADNY + SCHWARTZ
Cleveland, OH, USA
info@nsideas.com

NICOLE CHIALA DESIGN
Los Angeles, CA, USA
nixc@jps.net

NORTH BANK
Bath, United Kingdom
simon@northbankdesign.co.uk

PACEY + PACEY
North Vancouver, BC, Canada
paceyandpacey@hotmail.com

PAPER HAT DESIGN WORKS
San Francisco, CA, USA
tom.lyons@leagassf.com

PEPE GIMENO
Godelli, Spain
proyectografico@pepegimeno.com

PLATFORM CREATIVE GROUP
Seattle, WA, USA
cristy@platformcreative.com

PLUS DESIGN INC.
Boston, MA, USA
plus@plusdesigninc.com

POMEGRANATE
London, United Kingdom
shaun@pomegranate.co.uk

PUBLICIDAD GÓMEZ CHICA
Medellin, Columbia
sanjape@hotmail.com or
empaques@gomezchica.com.co

PURE DESIGN INC.
Portland, OR, USA
rachelle@puredesigninc.com

REACTOR ART + DESIGN
Toronto, ON, Canada
shari@reactor.ca

RED DESIGN
Brichton, United Kingdom
rachel@red-design.co.uk

RED STUDIOS
W. Hollywood, CA, USA
ruben@redstudios.com

RE: SALZMAN DESIGNS
Baltimore, MD, USA
ida.cheinman@verizon.net

RICK JOHNSON & CO.
Albuquerque, NM, USA
tmcgrath@rjc.com

THE RIORDON DESIGN GROUP
Oakville, ON, Canada
greer@riordondesign.com

RKS DESIGN
Thousand Oaks, CA, USA
ravi@rksdesign.com

ROBERT FROEDGE DESIGN
Franklin, TN, USA
robert@lewiscommunications.com

ROKFIL DESIGN
Mountain View, CA, USA
mbpdesign@hotmail.com

RUBIN CORDARO DESIGN
Minneapolis, MN, USA
j.cordaro@rubincordaro.com

SAGMEISTER, INC.
New York, NY, USA
ssagmeister@aol.com

SAYLES GRAPHIC DESIGN
Des Moines, IA, USA
sheree@saylesdesign.com

SMULLEN DESIGN

SPECIAL MODERN DESIGN
Los Angeles, CA, USA
kk@kbarranco.com

STILRADAR
Stuttgart, Germany
info@stilradar.de

STUDENT WORK
Kansas City, MO, USA
raka@uzigzag.com

TESSER, INC.
San Francisco, CA, USA
debra.naeve@tesser.com

THARP DID IT
Los Gatos, CA, USA

THE TOPLINE CORPORATION
Bellevue, WA, USA
cara_sanders@toplinecorp.com

THINKDESIGN & COMMUNICATIONS, INC.
Falls Church, VA, USA
jim@thinkdesign.net

TOM & JOHN: ADC
San Francisco, CA, USA
tom@tom-john.com

TOP DESIGN STUDIO
Toluca Lake, CA, USA
info@topdesign.com

TONG DESIGN
Tai Pei, Taiwan
tong8888@cm1.ethome.net.tw

TORNADO DESIGN
Los Angeles, CA, USA
alq@tornadodesign.la

UTILITY DESIGN
New York, NY, USA
www.utilitydesign.net

UP DESIGN BUREAU
Wichita, KS, USA
cp@vpdesignbureau.com

VRONTIKIS DESIGN OFFICE
Los Angeles, CA, USA
pv@35k.com

WALLACE CHURCH, INC.
New York, NY, USA
wendy@wallacechurch.com

WAVE 3
Louisville, KY, USA
art@wave3tv.com

WHY NOT ASSOCIATES
London, United Kingdom
info@whynotassociates.com

WILSON HARVEY
London, United Kingdom
paulb@wilsonharvey.co.uk

YES DESIGN
Glendale, CA, USA
yes-bas@pacbell.net

ZIGZAG DESIGN
Kansas City, MO, USA
raka@uzigzag.com

INDEX

SPECIAL THANKS TO:

Peleg Top for his vision, leadership, and inspiration,

Alexis Mercurio for her diligence, dedication, and talent,

Rebekah Beaton for her style and sophistication,

Shachar Lavi for her spirit and spunk,

Karen Shakarov for her passion and drive,

Molly Stretten for keeping us all in check,

Terese Harris for her efforts, precision, and lemon curd tarts,

Kristin Ellison for her confidence and assurance,

David Martinell for his direction and diplomacy,

Ricky Hoyt for his words and wisdom.